M000013396

how to solve

SHSAT

LOGICAL REASONING
PROBLEMS

STUDY GUIDE FOR THE NEW YORK CITY
SPECIALIZED HIGH SCHOOL ADMISSIONS TEST

STUYVESANT
BRONX SCIENCE
BROOKLYN TECH
STATEN ISLAND TECH

BROOKLYN LATIN
CITY COLLEGE
LEHMAN COLLEGE
YORK COLLEGE

· EXPERT STRATEGIES TO GIVE YOU THE EDGE
· 150 LOGICAL REASONING PROBLEMS
· DETAILED EXPLANATIONS

HOW TO SOLVE SHSAT LOGICAL REASONING PROBLEMS 2016

By the Staff of Five Points Learning Test Prep and Admissions

FIVE POINTS LEARNING

New York

© 2016 by Five Points Learning, Inc.
Published by Five Points Publishing, a division of Five Points Learning, Inc.
641 President Street, Suite 101
Brooklyn, NY 11215
E-mail: publisher@fivepointslearning.com

ISBN-10:0-9859660-3-3
ISBN-13:978-0-9859660-3-4

Printed in the United States of America
10 9 8 7 6 5 4 3 2 1
July 2016

Five Points Publishing books are available at special quantity discounts. For more information or to purchase books, please contact our special sales department at bulksales@fivepointslearning.com.

★ FIVE POINTS LEARNING

TABLE OF CONTENTS

—— INTRODUCTION

Congratulations on purchasing this logical reasoning practice book. Here is your opportunity to hone your skills on over a hundred logical reasoning practice questions. We have included a solution for each question, giving you the tools and strategies you need to boost your performance on the Verbal portion of the SHSAT.

So without further ado, let's cut to the chase.

The SHSAT has ten logical reasoning questions. The questions come in a variety of different flavors. Some will require you to draw diagrams, while others will require you to use your basic reasoning skills to figure out the correct answer.

We like to think of logical reasoning questions as games, similar to brain teasers. If you treat these questions like brain teasers, you may discover it's a lot easier to deal with the Logical Reasoning questions on the SHSAT.

In a moment, we'll discuss some specific strategies designed to assist you in tackling the common question types you'll encounter on the SHSAT. But first, you should be aware of how Logical Reasoning fits in with the rest of the test.

SHSAT STRUCTURE

The SHSAT is two and a half hours long and includes no breaks. This means you can take the test in any order you'd like. The test begins with the Verbal section, which consists of five Scrambled Paragraphs, ten Logical Reasoning questions, and six Reading Comprehension passages with five questions each. The second half of the test consists of fifty multiple-choice Math questions.

Your time management is vital if you want to score high on the SHSAT, so the order in which you take the test matters.

Whether you decide to do the Verbal section before or after the Math section is up to you. However, when it comes to the Verbal, we recommend you take on the Reading passages before you get to the Logical Reasoning or Scrambled Paragraphs questions.

Start with Reading because you have the potential to earn up to thirty raw points on the Reading passages alone. Logical Reasoning should follow Reading because you can earn up to ten raw points. Although Scrambled Paragraphs are worth two points apiece, they take a long time to solve, so do them last.

By spending the majority of your time on Math, Reading, and Logical Reasoning, you will maximize your potential to earn your highest score on the SHSAT.

THE IMPORTANCE OF TAKING GOOD NOTES

The purpose of Logical Reasoning questions is to confuse you. What's the easiest way to cancel out confusion? Use your pencil to take constant notes.

As you go through each problem, carefully write out the conditions on your scrap paper. Draw little symbols to represent each rule. Make the symbols as clear as possible. We recommend using letters and numbers.

We encourage you to practice this strategy by writing all over this book. Every time you solve a problem, show all your work. Don't solve anything in your head.

The purpose of this approach is to **NEVER** rely on your memory. If you try to solve logical reasoning questions in your head, you will continue to make careless mistakes and drag your score down. Always work out every question in your test book before you select the best answer choice.

This also applies to Reading Comprehension, Scrambled Paragraphs, and Math:

Write Everything Down!!!

PROCESS OF ELIMINATION

When it comes to answering multiple-choice questions, the process of elimination is your best friend.

Rather than trying to look for the right answer, we recommend looking for the wrong answers! Try to find flaws in four of the five options. Keep crossing out answers until you are left with the **LEAST** flawed option.

DON'T look at the answer choices until you understand every single condition mentioned in the problem. For example, if you're solving a Sequencing question, make sure you've determined the complete sequence as best you can before you select an option.

By fully working out the question before you look at the answers, your process of elimination will improve because you've already worked out the problem by yourself.

As you practice your process of elimination skills on these passages, check the solutions. Each solution indicates why certain answer choices are incorrect.

Now that we've covered the logical reasoning basics, let's take a look at the question types!

QUESTION TYPES

Code Games

You should always expect to see one code game on the SHSAT. It is among the most common logical reasoning question types.

In this question type, you will be presented with a code. The code will involve substituting words with letters. Your job is to determine which letters represent which words. Unlike on other logical reasoning questions, you will have to solve two code game questions per prompt.

Do **NOT** try to solve the entire code because you don't have enough time. Instead, focus only on the actual questions. You will only need to decode a couple of letters.

Make sure you read the instructions carefully. Here's an example of a typical Code Game prompt:

> **"In the code below, (1) each letter represents the same word in every sentence, (2) each word is always represented by only one letter, and (3) in any given sentence, the letters may or may not be presented in the same order as the words."**

Pay close attention to the third rule above. **"The letters may or may not be presented in the same order as the words."** *Always* check the third rule because this condition may not always be the same. For example, sometimes the letters can **NEVER** be in the same positions as the words they represent. If you misread the instructions, you will not be able to answer the questions correctly.

For Example…

Questions 1 and 2 refer to the following information.

In the code below, (1) each letter represents the same word in every sentence, (2) each word is always represented by only one letter, and (3) in any given sentence, the letters may or may not be presented in the same order as the words.

P	M	T	K	W	H	means
"Brenda	skis	in	the	cold	weather."	

K	P	X	H	M	S	means
"Matthew	rests	in	the	cold	weather."	

C	K	P	T	H	S	means
"Brenda	rests	in	the	hot	weather."	

H	N	K	C	P	X	means
"Matthew	swims	in	the	hot	weather."	

T	V	H	R	U	C	means
"Hot	weather	makes	Brenda	very	tired."	

1. Which letter represents the word "Brenda"?
   A. V
   B. H
   C. C
   D. M
   E. T

First, let's identify the sentences in which "Brenda" appears.

This word only appears in sentences 1, 3, and 5.

Next, let's go to the answer choices. Each answer choice gives you a letter. Compare each letter to the three sentences. Eliminate any answer choices that do not appear only in sentences 1, 3, and 5.

- The letter V only appears in sentence 5. Cross it out.
- The letter H appears in all five sentences, but "Brenda" does not. Cross it out.
- The letter C appears in sentences 3, 4, and 5. Cross it out.
- The letter M appears in sentences 1 and 2 only. Cross it out.
- This leaves us with the letter T. The letter T appears only in sentences 1, 3, and 5. Therefore, Option E is the correct answer.

Let's try another problem!

2. Which word is represented by the letter V?
　　F. hot
　　G. makes
　　H. very
　　J. tired
　　K. Cannot be determined from the information given.

Now, do the same thing with the letter V. This time, however, we are trying to figure out which word the letter V represents.

We already know based on Question 1 that the letter V only appears in sentence 5. So let's review the answer choices. Any word that does not appear only in sentence 5 cannot be correct.

- The word "hot" appears in sentences 3, 4, and 5. Cross it out.
- The words "makes," "very," and "tired" also appear only in sentence 5.
- The letters R and U also appear only in sentence 5. Thus any of these options could be correct.

Therefore, the correct answer is Option K: "Cannot be determined from the information given."

NOTE: Students often assume that "Cannot be determined from the information given" is a trap answer. However, sometimes "Cannot be determined" is correct!

CODE GAMES PRACTICE QUIZ

Questions 1 and 2 refer to the following information.

In the code below, (1) each letter represents the same word in every sentence, (2) each word is always represented by only one letter, and (3) in any given sentence, the letters may or may not be presented in the same order as the words.

D	V	M	S	J	C	means
"Janet	runs	over	the	green	grass."	
M	D	V	R	C	K	means
"Janet	runs	through	the	green	bush."	
M	J	T	L	V	S	means
"Mike	runs	over	the	brown	grass."	
J	T	V	D	M	R	means
"Janet	runs	over	the	brown	bush."	
V	L	M	C	R	K	means
"Mike	runs	through	the	green	bush."	

1. Which letter represents the word "grass"?
   A. D
   B. K
   C. M
   D. V
   E. S

2. Which word is represented by the letter T?
   F. Janet
   G. the
   H. brown
   J. over
   K. bush

Questions 3 and 4 refer to the following information.

In the code below, (1) each letter represents the same word in every sentence, (2) each word is always represented by only one letter, and (3) in any given sentence, the letters may or may not be presented in the same order as the words.

T	P	L	D	G	X	means
"Jason	jumped	over	the	burning	candlestick."	

P	T	X	M	D	K	means
"Jack	jumped	over	the	unlit	candlestick."	

J	N	P	G	X	D	means
"John	tripped	over	the	burning	candlestick."	

X	W	L	J	C	P	means
"Jason	tripped	over	the	brown	rug."	

D	X	G	R	X	C	means
"The	burning	candlestick	singed	the	rug."	

3. Which word is represented by the letter R?
   A. singed
   B. the
   C. burning
   D. candlestick
   E. rug

4. Which letter represents the word "unlit"?
   F. J
   G. P
   H. T
   J. X
   K. K

Questions 5 and 6 refer to the following information.

In the code below, (1) each letter represents the same word in every sentence, (2) each word is always represented by only one letter, and (3) in any given sentence, the letters may or may not be presented in the same order as the words.

T	X	L	H	O	D	means
"Dogs	bark	loudly	at	the	moon."	
H	**L**	**K**	**V**	**X**	**T**	means
"Dogs	bark	softly	at	the	sun."	
D	**H**	**R**	**B**	**W**	**L**	means
"Dogs	snarl	loudly	towards	the	cats."	
H	**K**	**S**	**Q**	**V**	**R**	means
"Cats	purr	softly	in	the	sun."	
V	**Y**	**L**	**E**	**S**	**H**	means
"Dogs	yelp	softly	in	the	cold."	

5. Which word is represented by the letter T?
- A. dogs
- B. bark
- C. loudly
- D. moon
- E. sun

6. Which letter represents the word "snarl"?
- F. T
- G. W
- H. K
- J. B
- K. Cannot be determined from the information given.

CODE GAMES PRACTICE QUIZ SOLUTIONS

1. **E** The word "grass" appears in sentences 1 and 3 only. The letter S appears in sentences 1 and 3 only. There are no other words or letters that appear only in sentences 1 and 3. Therefore, S must represent "grass."

2. **H** The letter T appears in sentences 3 and 4. The word "brown" also only appears in sentences 3 and 4. No other words or letters appear only in sentences 3 and 4. Option F is incorrect because "Janet" appears in sentences 1, 2 and 3. Option G is incorrect because "the" appears in all five of the sentences. Option J is incorrect because "over" appears in sentence 1 as well as sentences 3 and 4. Option K is incorrect because "bush" appears in sentences 4 and 5, and T appears only in sentences 3 and 4.

3. **A** R appears only in sentence 5. The word "singed" also appears only in sentence 5. No other letters or words appear exclusively in sentence 5. Thus R must represent "singed." All the other answer choices appear in other sentences.

4. **K** "Unlit" appears only in sentence 2, which is the only sentence where you'll see the letter K. All the other options appear in multiple sentences besides sentence 2.

5. **B** The letter T appears only in sentences 1 and 2. The word "barks" is the only word that appears in sentences 1 and 2 but no other. Option A is incorrect because "dogs" appears in sentences 1, 2, 3, and 5. Option C is incorrect because "loudly" appears in sentences 1 and 3, not sentences 1 and 2. Option D is incorrect because "moon" appears only in sentence 1 and not in sentence 2. Option E is incorrect because "sun" appears in sentences 2 and 4, not sentences 1 and 2.

6. **K** "Snarl" appears only in sentence 3. The word "towards" also appears only in sentence 3. In addition, the letters W and B only appear in this sentence. There is nothing in the code that allows you to determine which letter represents which word. Therefore, Option K is correct.

SEQUENCING GAMES

Sequencing games will ask you to determine the correct order of a particular sequence. These sequences may involve people standing in a line, or they may involve a row of objects such as hats or books.

Follow each rule carefully. Draw out a diagram for each rule before you attempt to put the sequence together. Don't answer the question until the sequence is as complete as possible.

For Example...

1. Oscar has an after-school job stacking books in the library. On one shelf he organizes five books according to height, from shortest to tallest.

   1) The brown book is taller than the red book, which is taller than the blue book.
   2) The black book is shorter than the brown book but taller than the green book.
   3) The green book is shorter than the red book but taller than the blue book.

Before we reveal the question, start to work out the sequence by drawing a little diagram for each rule:

RULE 1: The brown book is taller than the red book, which is taller than the blue book.

DIAGRAM: Brown → Red → Blue

RULE 2: The black book is shorter than the brown book but taller than the green book.

DIAGRAM: Brown → Black → Green

RULE 3:   The green book is shorter than the red book but taller than the blue book.

DIAGRAM: Red → Green → Blue

Next, we need to put the three diagrams together for the complete sequence. In this problem, we have not been provided with the relationship between the red book and the black book. However, both books are shorter than the brown book and taller than the green book. Therefore, the problem results in **TWO** possible sequences:

Brown → Red → Black → Green → Blue

OR

Brown → Black → Red → Green → Blue

Now, let's take a look at the question:

Which book is the fourth tallest?
   A. brown
   B. red
   C. green
   D. black
   E. Cannot be determined from the information given.

In both possible sequences, the green book is the fourth tallest. Therefore, Option C must be correct.

Let's try another problem!

2.   Mitch is a singer who is looking for a guitar accompanist. He makes a list of all the guitar players he knows and ranks them in order of preference.

   1)   Julie is a better guitar player than Sandy and Beth.
   2)   Michelle is a better guitar player than Sandy.
   3)   Annie is a better guitar player than Michelle, but is not as good as Julie.

This time, draw the diagrams yourself. Remember: Keep them simple!

RULE 1: Julie is a better guitar player than Sandy and Beth.
DIAGRAM:

RULE 2: Michelle is a better guitar player than Sandy.
DIAGRAM:

RULE 3: Annie is a better guitar player than Michelle, but is not as good as Julie.
DIAGRAM:

Now put the three diagrams together for the complete sequence.
COMPLETE DIAGRAM:

Your diagrams for each rule should look something like the figures below.

Rule 1: Julie is a better guitar player than Sandy and Beth.

$$Julie \nearrow^{Beth}_{\searrow Sandy}$$

Rule 2: Michelle is a better guitar player than Sandy.

$$Michelle \rightarrow Sandy$$

Rule 3: Annie is a better guitar player than Michelle, but is not as good as Julie.

$$Julie \rightarrow Annie \rightarrow Michelle$$

With this piece of information, we can put the above sequences together:

$$Julie \rightarrow Annie \rightarrow Michelle \rightarrow Sandy \\ \searrow Beth$$

Now, let's take a look at the question.

Which guitar player does Mitch like the best?
- F.   Julie
- G.   Sandy
- H.   Beth
- J.   Michelle
- K.   Annie

We know that Mitch likes Julie more than Beth according to Rule 1, but there is not enough information to place Beth in the sequence definitively. Sandy is the guitar player Mitch likes the least. Annie is the second favorite guitar player, and Michelle is the third favorite guitar player.

Your diagrams should have revealed that Mitch likes Julie's guitar playing the best. Therefore, Option F is the correct answer.

SEQUENCING GAMES PRACTICE QUIZ

1. Malcolm loves playing sports. He decides to rank his five favorite sports.

   1) Malcolm likes golf more than bowling but less than baseball.
   2) Malcolm likes football more than soccer.
   3) Malcolm likes bowling more than football.

What is Malcolm's second favorite sport?
   A. golf
   B. bowling
   C. baseball
   D. football
   E. soccer

2. A hospital created a work schedule in which each nurse would work only one day, from Wednesday through Saturday.

   1) Nurse Frances was originally scheduled to work on Wednesday, but she traded with Nurse George, who was scheduled to work on Friday.
   2) Nurse Jane traded with Nurse Kris, who was scheduled to work on Saturday.

Which nurse worked on Thursday?
   F. Nurse Frances
   G. Nurse George
   H. Nurse Jane
   J. Nurse Kris
   K. Cannot be determined from the information given.

3. There are five race cars of different colors taking part in a big race. The cars are red, blue, yellow, green, and purple.

1) The green car finished the race before the red car.
2) The yellow car finished directly behind the red one.
3) The purple car did not finish in first place.
4) The car that finished last was neither red nor green nor blue.

In which place did the blue car finish?
A. first
B. second
C. third
D. fourth
E. fifth

SEQUENCING GAMES PRACTICE QUIZ SOLUTIONS

1. **A** Draw a diagram for each rule so that you can work out the sequence carefully. Rule 1 tells us that Malcolm ranks golf between bowling and baseball:

    Baseball → Golf → Bowling

    Rule 2 tells us that Malcolm likes football more than he likes soccer, but we don't know how these sports relate to the others. So all we can draw thus far is this:

    Football → Soccer

    Rule 3 compares football to bowling. This rule allows us to rank all of the sports. Because Malcolm prefers bowling to football and football to soccer, we know that football and soccer must be ranked fourth and fifth, respectively:

    Baseball → Golf → Bowling → Football → Soccer

    Therefore, Malcolm's second favorite sport is golf.

2. **J** First, draw a diagram like the one below. This will help you keep the information about the nurses organized:

Wednesday	Thursday	Friday	Saturday

    Start by writing in the shifts assigned to Nurse Frances and Nurse George, as per Rule 1. Since the two have switched days, Nurse George works on Wednesday and Nurse Frances works on Friday.

Wednesday	Thursday	Friday	Saturday
Georges		Frances	

Next, look at Rule 2. We know that Nurse Kris swapped with Nurse Jane. If Nurse Kris was originally scheduled to work on Saturday, then she must be working on Thursday now. Therefore, Nurse Jane is working on Saturday and Nurse Kris is working on Thursday. This sequence is represented by Option J:

Wednesday	Thursday	Friday	Saturday
Georges	Kris	Frances	Jane

3. **D** The first two conditions tell us that the green car finished before the red car and that the red car finished before the yellow car.

Green → Red → Yellow

Rule 4 tells us that the car in last place was neither red nor green nor blue, which means it was either yellow or purple. But since the yellow car was directly behind the red car according to Rule 2, we know the yellow car did not finish last. This means that the purple car must have finished in fifth, and the blue car must have finished in fourth place:

Green → Red → Yellow → Blue → Purple

The question is asking for the position of the blue car. According to the diagram above, Option D is the correct answer.

MATCHING GAMES

Matching games will test your ability to match people, places, or objects with the correct characteristics that describe them.

As with sequencing games, your success on matching games will rest upon your willingness to take notes and create diagrams in order to keep the information organized.

NEVER attempt to answer the question until you have correctly matched up all the characteristics with their subjects.

For Example...

1. At the Bay Park library, two posters encouraging children to read are hanging above the checkout desk.

   1) One poster features a cartoon lion holding a book.
   2) One poster includes a large plant.
   3) The poster featuring a famous athlete holding up a book uses yellow-colored letters.
   4) The poster using orange-colored letters does not include a large plant and features the book *The Adventures of Tom Sawyer*.
   5) The famous athlete is holding up a copy of *Wuthering Heights*.
   6) The lion poster includes a bookshelf.

Let's start by making a chart for the two posters. Include two columns: one for the Lion poster and one for the Athlete poster. Fill in each row one at a time:

Lion	Athlete

According to Rules 3 and 4, the athlete poster uses yellow letters. This means the lion poster must use orange letters. Rule 4 also tells us that the lion poster includes the book *The Adventures of Tom Sawyer*.

Lion	Athlete
Orange Letters	Yellow Letters
Tom Sawyer	

Rule 5 tells us that the athlete is holding up a copy of *Wuthering Heights*. Write that into your chart next. Rule 6 tells us that the lion poster includes a bookshelf. Finally, refer back to Rules 2 and 4. If the lion poster does not include the large plant, then it follows that the athlete poster includes the large plant.

Lion	Athlete
Orange Letters	Yellow Letters
Tom Sawyer	Wuthering Heights
Bookshelf	Large Plant

We can now answer the question:

Based only on the information above, which of the following MUST be true?
  A. The lion poster uses yellow letters.
  B. The lion poster features the book The Adventures of Tom Sawyer.
  C. The lion poster features the book Wuthering Heights.
  D. The athlete poster uses orange letters.
  E. Cannot be determined from the information given.

Options A, C, and D are incorrect. The only answer choice that agrees with the diagram is Option B, which is the correct answer.

Let's try another problem!

2. Haig, Randall, Gareth, and Ajani go to a used video store. Each person purchases a DVD from a different genre.

    1) Ajani purchases the war movie.
    2) Randall does not purchase the adventure movie or the horror movie.
    3) Gareth does not purchase the horror movie.

What is the genre of the movie Haig purchases?

F. adventure
G. comedy
H. horror
J. war
K. Cannot be determined from the information given.

Use the space below to create your own diagram:

According to Rule 1, Ajani purchased the war movie. Rule 2 states that Randall did not purchase the adventure movie or the horror movie. This means he must have purchased the comedy movie. Rule 3 states that Gareth did not purchase the horror movie. This means that Gareth must have purchased the adventure movie, and Haig must have purchased the horror movie. Therefore, Option H is the correct answer.

This is what your completed chart should look like:

Haig	Randall	Gareth	Ajani
Horror	Comedy	Adventure	War

MATCHING GAMES PRACTICE QUIZ

1. Kate, Joanna, Nina, and Bonnie take a trip to a farmer's market. Each goes home with a basket containing a different vegetable: avocados, carrots, celery, and strawberries.

1) Either Kate or Bonnie has the basket with avocados.
2) Joanna has the basket with strawberries.
3) Nina does not have avocados or celery.

Who has the basket with carrots?
A. Bonnie
B. Joanna
C. Kate
D. Nina
E. Cannot be determined from the information given.

2. Francisco goes to a deli and orders two sandwiches for lunch and dinner, respectively.

1) One sandwich is a hero while the other sandwich is on a roll.
2) One sandwich is vegetarian and includes cheese.
3) The sandwich that does not include cheese is a turkey sandwich.
4) The hero does not include mayonnaise, but it does include salt and pepper.
5) The turkey sandwich is on a roll and includes both mayonnaise and ketchup.

Based only on the information above, which of the following MUST be true?
F. The turkey sandwich does not include cheese.
G. The turkey sandwich contains salt and pepper.
H. The vegetarian sandwich is on a roll.
J. The vegetarian sandwich does not include cheese.
K. Cannot be determined from the information given.

3. Five friends travel to different European cities for their summer vacations. The cities visited are Paris, London, Dublin, Barcelona, and Venice.

1) Vince went to London.
2) Julian either went to Barcelona or Paris.
3) Marc did not go to Paris, Barcelona, or Venice.
4) Howard either went to Venice or Dublin.
5) Noel did not go to Barcelona.

Which city did Noel visit?

A. Barcelona
B. Dublin
C. Paris
D. Venice
E. Cannot be determined from the information given.

MATCHING GAMES PRACTICE QUIZ SOLUTIONS

1. **D** Draw a diagram like the one below. According to Rule 2, Joanna brought the strawberries home. Since this is the clearest piece of information in the conditions, write this into the diagram first. Rule 3 tells us that Nina did not bring home either avocados or strawberries. This means she must have brought home carrots. We know based on Rule 1 that either Kate or Bonnie brought home the avocados. However, there is not enough information to determine who purchased the avocados or the celery.

Kate	Joanna	Nina	Bonnie
Avocados/ Celery	Strawberries	Carrots	Celery/ Avocados

The question is asking for the person with the basket containing carrots. Option D is correct.

2. **F** Draw a diagram like the one below. Start with the clearest piece of information provided. Rule 5 tells us that the sandwich on a roll is a turkey sandwich that includes mayonnaise and ketchup. This means that the hero must be the vegetarian sandwich. According to Rules 2 and 4, the vegetarian sandwich includes cheese as well as salt and pepper, but not mayonnaise.

Hero	Roll
Vegetarian	Turkey
Cheese	No Cheese
No Mayonnaise	Mayonnaise
Salt & Pepper	Ketchup

After you've completed your diagram, compare the data to the answer choices. The only answer choice that is supported by the information provided is Option F.

3. **C** Draw a diagram like the one below. The clearest piece of information is that Vince went to London, which is stated in Rule 1. Write this piece of information into the diagram first. Now go through each rule and see if you can deduce who went to which city. According to Rule 3, Marc did not go to Paris, Barcelona, or Venice. Since he also didn't go to London, Marc must have gone to Dublin. Rule 4 tells us that Howard either went to Venice or Dublin. Based on these two rules, we can determine that Howard went to Venice. Rule 2 states that Julian went to either Paris or Barcelona. However, Rule 5 states that Noel did not go to Barcelona. This means that Julian must have gone to Barcelona and Noel must have gone to Paris. Option C is the correct answer.

Paris	London	Dublin	Barcelona	Venice
Noel	Vince	Marc	Julian	Howard

SEQUENCING/MATCHING GAMES

Sequencing/Matching games combine the joys of both sequencing and matching questions.

Although these games may seem more difficult from the outset, they can still be solved by creating diagrams and carefully filling them in.

We suggest that on any sequencing/matching game, you focus on one component at a time. On some questions, it might be easier to start with the matching element. On other questions, however, the sequencing component may be simpler to start with.

For Example...

1. Five student-athletes—Fred, James, Warren, Donna, and Adam—are standing in the cafeteria line. Each student plays a different sport.

   1) James is in the fourth position and plays soccer.
   2) There are exactly three students between the football player and the baseball player.
   3) Fred and Warren are in front of the tennis and soccer players.
   4) The basketball player is second in line.
   5) Adam plays baseball.
   6) The soccer player is in between the tennis player and the baseball player.

Before we take a look at the question, let's draw a diagram to organize all the information above. The diagram will consist of two rows—one for student name and one for the sport played—and five columns, one for each of the five students.

Rule 1 tells us that James is in the fourth position and plays soccer, so let's fill that in first. Rule 4 tells us that the basketball player is second in line; so we can fill that in next. Rule 2 tells us that there are exactly three students between the football and baseball player. Although their positions are currently unclear, we can nevertheless deduce that these players are in the first and fifth positions, respectively. This is what our diagram looks like so far:

			James	
Football/ Baseball	Basketball		Soccer	Baseball/ Football

Rule 3 tells us that Fred and Warren are in front of the tennis and soccer players. This puts them in the first and second positions. It is unclear who is in which position. Rule 6 tells us that the soccer player is in between the tennis player and the baseball player. This allows us to determine that the tennis player is in the third position, the baseball player is in the fifth position, and the football player is in the first position. Rule 5 tells us that Adam plays baseball. The only player left is Donna, who must be the tennis player.

Fred/ Warren	Warren/ Fred	Donna	James	Adam
Football	Basketball	Tennis	Soccer	Baseball

Finally, let's take a look at the question:

1. What does the student in the fifth position play?
>   A. baseball
>   B. basketball
>   C. soccer
>   D. tennis
>   E. Cannot be determined from the information given.

Adam is in the fifth position and plays baseball. Therefore, Option A is correct.

Let's try another problem!

2. Alfred, Beth, Crispin, Dayna, and Eugene all have to present book reports. Each student will present a book report on a different school day.

    1) The student who read *Oliver Twist* presents the book report on Tuesday.
    2) Three book reports are presented between Beth and Crispin's book reports.
    3) The book report on *Cyrano De Bergerac* is presented the day after the book report on *The Red Badge of Courage*.
    4) Beth presents her book report on *The Odyssey* on Friday.
    5) Dayna presents her book report on Thursday.
    6) The book report on *Romeo & Juliet* is presented two days before the book report on *The Red Badge of Courage*.
    7) Alfred presents his book report the day before Eugene's book report.

Who presented the book report on Cyrano De Bergerac?
    F. Alfred
    G. Crispin
    H. Dayna
    J. Eugene
    K. Cannot be determined from the information given.

First, we need to draw a diagram consisting of five columns and two rows. On the top row, we'll write in the names of the students. On the bottom row, we'll write in the names of the books.

According to Rule 1, the *Oliver Twist* report was presented on Tuesday. Write this book into Position 2 on the bottom row. Next, look at Rule 4. This rule tells us that Beth presented her report on *The Odyssey* on Friday. Write this into the diagram. Rule 5 tells us that Dayna presented her report on Thursday. According to Rule 2, three book reports are presented between those of Beth and Crispin. Thus, Crispin's book report must have been presented on Monday:

Crispin			Dayna	Beth
	Oliver Twist			The Odyssey

Now we need to determine the order of Eugene and Alfred. According to Rule 7, Alfred presented his book report the day before Eugene's. This places Alfred in Position 2 and Eugene in Position 3.

Finally, we need to match up the students with the rest of the books. Rule 6 tells us that the *Romeo & Juliet* book report is presented two days before that of *The Red Badge of Courage*. Rule 3 tells us that the book report on *Cyrano De Bergerac* took place the day after *The Red Badge of Courage* book report. Therefore, *Romeo & Juliet* was presented on Monday, *The Red Badge of Courage* was presented on Wednesday, and *Cyrano De Bergerac* was presented on Thursday.

Crispin	Alfred	Eugene	Dayna	Beth
Romeo & Juliet	Oliver Twist	The Red Badge of Courage	Cyrano De Bergerac	The Odyssey

The question is asking for who presented the book report on *Cyrano De Bergerac*. Option H, Dayna, is the correct answer.

SEQUENCING/MATCHING GAMES PRACTICE QUIZ

1. At a banquet hall, there are five different colored tables lined up from front to back. Each table displays a different type of food.

    1) The table displaying cheese comes before the table displaying meat.
    2) The orange table is last.
    3) The green table comes after the blue table but before the red table.
    4) The table displaying fruit comes directly after the green table and directly before the red table.
    5) The yellow table comes before the table displaying vegetables.
    6) The red table is displaying bread.

    Which table is in the second position?
    A. cheese
    B. fruit
    C. meat
    D. vegetables
    E. Cannot be determined from the information given.

2. Four cleaners—Wanda, Mitch, Val, and Zoe—are cleaning an office. Each performs one job only. The jobs are dusting, vacuuming, washing windows, and emptying trash.

    1) Wanda washes windows before Val completes his job and is not in the fourth position.
    2) Val works immediately after the cleaner who dusts.
    3) Mitch completes his job before Wanda does hers.

    Based only on the information above, which of the following MUST be true?
    F. Wanda cleans first.
    G. Val cleans last.
    H. Zoe cleans last.
    J. Val cleans first.
    K. Zoe cleans before Mitch.

3. In a canoe race, four canoes cross the finish line. There are no ties. The canoes represent four different high schools: Jefferson, Kennedy, Franklin, and Washington. The colors of the canoes are red, yellow, blue, and green.

    1) The yellow canoe finished before the green canoe.
    2) Franklin High School raced the yellow canoe.
    3) Kennedy High School raced the red canoe and finished directly after Jefferson High School.
    4) Jefferson High School finished directly after Washington High School.
    5) Washington High School did not race the green canoe.

Which school won the race?
    A. Kennedy High School
    B. Washington High School
    C. Franklin High School
    D. Jefferson High School
    E. Cannot be determined from the information given.

4. Five shoppers are waiting in line at a grocery store: Michelle, Ralph, Watson, Cindy, and Robin. Each shopper is buying a different item.

    1) Cindy is last in line.
    2) The shopper buying pastrami is behind the person buying ham.
    3) Watson is ahead of Robin and Michelle.
    4) The shopper buying Colby cheese is in the fourth position
    5) The shopper buying cheddar cheese is first in line.
    6) Robin is buying a turkey and is directly behind Ralph.
    7) Michelle is buying Colby cheese.

Based only on the information above, which of the following MUST be true?
    F. Cindy is buying pastrami.
    G. Ralph is buying cheddar cheese.
    H. Watson is buying cheddar cheese.
    J. Michelle is last in line.
    K. Robin is first in line.

SEQUENCING/MATCHING GAMES PRACTICE QUIZ SOLUTIONS

1. **C** Draw a diagram like the one below. Start with the clearest piece of information. Rule 2 tells us that the orange table is last, so write that into the diagram first. We also know based on Rule 3 that the blue table is before the green table and that the green table comes before the red table. However, we do not know where the yellow table is. Let's take a look at Rule 4. This rule states that the table displaying fruit comes directly after the green table and directly before the red table. This must be the yellow table as the blue table has to come before the green table according to Rule 3:

Blue	Green	Yellow	Red	Orange
		Fruit		

Next, we need to match the rest of the foods with their tables. Rule 6 tells us that the red table is displaying bread, so fill that in first. Rule 5 tells us that the yellow table comes before the vegetable table. This means that the vegetables must be on the orange table. Finally, Rule 1 tells us that the cheese table comes before the meat table. This means that the cheese is in the first position, and the meat is in the second position:

Blue	Green	Yellow	Red	Orange
Cheese	Meat	Fruit	Bread	Vegetables

2. **G** Draw a diagram like the one below. According to Rule 1, Wanda washes the windows and is not last. According to Rule 3, Mitch cleans before Wanda. This means Wanda must clean second or third. According to Rule 2, Val has to clean immediately after the cleaner who dusts. This means Wanda cannot be third because Wanda washes the windows. Wanda cleans second, the cleaner who dusts is third, and Val cleans last. Mitch is first and Zoe, who dusts, must be third. It is unclear who vacuums or empties the trash, but Mitch and Val must each perform one of these tasks.

Mitch	**Wanda**	**Zoe**	**Val**
Vacuum/Trash	Windows	Dusting	Trash/Vacuum

Based on the data above, Option G must be correct.

3. **C** Draw a diagram like the one below. Rules 3 and 4 tell us that Jefferson finished immediately after Washington but before Kennedy. To determine their exact positions in the sequence, look at Rules 1 and 2. Franklin raced the yellow canoe and came in before at least one other canoe, the green one. Thus Franklin must be in first place, and the other three schools are in the following three positions.

Franklin	**Washington**	**Jefferson**	**Kennedy**
Yellow			

According to Rule 3, Kennedy raced the red canoe. Rule 5 tells us that Washington did not race the green canoe. Therefore, it must have raced the blue canoe. Jefferson must have placed third with the green canoe.

Franklin	**Washington**	**Jefferson**	**Kennedy**
Yellow	Blue	Green	Red

The question is asking for the school that won the race. Option C is the correct answer.

4. **F** Draw a diagram like the one below. Rule 1 tells us that Cindy is last in line, so fill that in first. Rule 5 states that the first shopper is buying cheddar, so fill "cheddar" into the first column accordingly. Rule 3 tells us that Watson comes before Robin and Michelle. Rule 6 tells us that Robin is buying a turkey and is directly behind Ralph. This means that Watson must also be ahead of Ralph. Based on this, we can determine that Watson is in the first position. Rule 7 tells us that Michelle is buying Colby cheese. This means that Michelle has to be in the fourth position. Thus Ralph is in the second position and Robin is in the third position. Finally, we need to determine who is buying pastrami and who is buying ham. According to Rule 2, the shopper buying pastrami is behind the shopper buying ham. Since Cindy is in the last position, she must be buying pastrami and Ralph must be buying ham.

Watson	Ralph	Robin	Michelle	Cindy
Cheddar	Ham	Turkey	Colby	Pastrami

Compare the answer choices to the information in the diagram above. Option F is the correct answer.

IF/THEN GAMES

If/Then games are a fairly common question type in the Logical Reasoning section of the test. Luckily, these games can be solved by using a simple and easy-to-remember approach.

Every If/Then statement will present one condition that is dependent upon another condition:

If it is bright outside, then the sun is out.

The question will then ask you to select the only answer choice that **must** be true according to the information provided.

In order to solve any If/Then game, all you need to do is take the original statement and form its **contrapositive**.

The contrapositive of any given statement is formed by reversing the two conditions and negating them.

This simple, two-step approach will convert the original statement into the contrapositive, which is the **ONLY** statement that must be true based on the information given.

If it is <u>bright</u> outside, then the sun is <u>out</u>.

BECOMES...

If the sun is <u>not out</u>, then it is <u>not bright</u> outside.

Once you form the contrapositive, go to the answer choices and find out which option best matches up with the contrapositive answer. This will always be the correct answer for If/Then Games.

For Example...

1. If dresses are on sale, then Mary will replace her wardrobe.

Based only on the information above, which of the following MUST be true?
A. Mary can afford to replace her wardrobe only if dresses are on sale.
B. Whenever dresses are on sale, Mary buys as many as possible.
C. If dresses are not on sale, then Mary will not replace her wardrobe.
D. Mary will not replace her wardrobe if dresses are not on sale.
E. Mary will not replace her wardrobe only if dresses are on sale.

First of all, let's take the original statement and form the contrapositive. Remember: Reverse the conditions and negate!

If dresses are <u>on sale</u>, then Mary will <u>replace her wardrobe</u>.

BECOMES...

If Mary does <u>not replace her wardrobe</u>, then dresses are <u>not on sale</u>.

Now, let's compare our contrapositive statement to the answer choices:

- Option A is an extreme answer. The question never states that Mary can only afford to replace her wardrobe if dresses are on sale.
- Option B is an assumption. The question never states that Mary will buy as many dresses as possible.
- Option C negates the clauses without reversing them. Mary may replace her wardrobe under a different set of circumstances.
- Option D reverses the two clauses and negates them. Let's hold onto this one.
- Option E is both an extreme statement and an assumption. The question never suggests that a sale on dresses makes Mary less likely to replace her wardrobe.

The only answer choice that fulfills the conditions of the contrapositive is Option D. Therefore, it is correct.

Now, some If/Then games require a little more work. In certain cases, If/Then games may consist of two sentences as opposed to one.

Let's try another problem!

2. If you play piano, then you enjoy music. If you sing in the shower, then you enjoy music.

   Based only on the information above, which of the following MUST be true?
   F. People who enjoy music play the piano.
   G. People who enjoy music sing in the shower.
   H. People who sing in the shower do not play the piano.
   J. If you do not sing in the shower, you do not play the piano.
   K. If you do not enjoy music, then you do not play the piano, and you do not sing in the shower.

First of all, notice that the two sentences have one clause in common: "You enjoy music."

This means that before we form the contrapositive, we can combine the two sentences into one If/Then statement:

If you play the piano and sing in the shower, then you enjoy music.

Now, just like we did on the last problem, let's take the If/Then statement and form the contrapositive.

If you play the piano and sing in the shower, then you enjoy music.

BECOMES...

**If you do not enjoy music, then you do not play the piano,
and you do not sing in the shower.**

Finally, we can compare the answer choices.

- Option F is an assumption. Not everyone who enjoys music necessarily plays the piano.
- Option G is an assumption. Not everyone who enjoys music necessarily sings in the shower.
- Option H is an assumption. We don't have any information to support this answer.
- Option J negates the statements and is presented in the If/Then format. However, this statement is not necessarily true. The original statement does not indicate a direct relationship between singing in the shower and playing the piano.
- Option K reverses the clauses and negates them. It is presented in the correct contrapositive form. Therefore, it is the correct answer.

QUICK TIP: Always assume that the original If/Then statement is true. Never assume anything that isn't supported by either the original statement or the contrapositive.

IF/THEN GAMES PRACTICE QUIZ

1. If you study Logical Reasoning, then you will raise your Verbal score.

   Based only on the information above, which of the following MUST be true?
   A. If you raise your Verbal score, then you studied Logical Reasoning.
   B. If you do not study Logical Reasoning, then you will not raise your Verbal score.
   C. If you do not raise your Verbal score, then you did not study Logical Reasoning.
   D. To understand Logical Reasoning, then you must have a logical mind.
   E. If you raise your Verbal score, then you did not study Logical Reasoning.

2. If the leaves are falling, then it is autumn.

   Based only on the information above, which of the following MUST be true?
   F. If it is not autumn, then the leaves are not falling.
   G. If the leaves are not falling, then it is not autumn.
   H. If it is autumn, then there are no leaves on the trees.
   J. If the leaves are falling, then it will snow soon.
   K. If the leaves are falling, then somebody needs to rake the leaves.

3. If Calvin ate the pizza, then it was a cheese pizza. If Calvin ate the pizza, it was from Rocco's Pizzeria.

   Based only on the information above, which of the following MUST be true?
   A. If the pizza was a cheese pizza, then Calvin ate it.
   B. If the pizza was not from Rocco's Pizzeria, then Calvin did not eat it.
   C. If Calvin did not eat the pizza, then it was not from Rocco's Pizzeria.
   D. If the pizza was not a cheese pizza, then it was not from Rocco's Pizzeria.
   E. If the pizza was from Rocco's Pizzeria, then Calvin ate it.

4. If you love fashion, then you will love shopping. If you love shopping, then you like to spend a lot of money.

Based only on the information above, which of the following MUST be true?

   F. If you love fashion, then you will not spend a lot of money.

   G. If you like to spend a lot of money, then you love fashion.

   H. If you like to spend a lot of money, then you love shopping.

   J. If you do not love fashion, then you do not like to spend a lot of money.

   K. If you do not like to spend a lot of money, then you do not love shopping.

IF/THEN GAMES PRACTICE QUIZ SOLUTIONS

1. **C** First, form the contrapositive by flipping the two clauses and then negating them. The contrapositive is as follows:

   "If you do not raise your Verbal score, then you did not study Logical Reasoning."

   The only answer choice that fulfills the conditions of the contrapositive is Option C. Option A is incorrect because a student may still raise his or her Verbal score without studying Logical Reasoning (although we do not advise this!). Option B is an extreme assumption that is not supported by the information provided. Option D introduces outside information by mentioning a "logical mind." Option E is also an assumption that is not supported by the information provided.

2. **F** Flip the two statements and negate them to form the contrapositive:

   "If it is not autumn, then the leaves are not falling."

   Option F must be correct because it follows the contrapositive exactly. Option G can be ruled out because other circumstances could result in the leaves falling. All the other options can be ruled out because they introduce outside information that isn't supported by the information provided.

3. **B**   Combine the two statements by linking them with the shared clause, "If Calvin ate the pizza."

"If Calvin ate the pizza, then it was a cheese pizza, and it was from Rocco's Pizzeria."

Now, flip the clauses and negate them to form the contrapositive:

"If the pizza was not from Rocco's Pizzeria and was not a cheese pizza, then Calvin did not eat the pizza."

The only option that follows the conditions of the contrapositive is Option B. Option A is not necessarily true because, based on this statement, all cheese pizzas will be eaten by Calvin. Option C is incorrect because other circumstances may have dissuaded Calvin from eating the pizza. Options D and E are assumptions that are not supported by either the original statement or the contrapositive.

4. **K**   First, combine the sentences. Then, form the contrapositive by reversing the clauses and then negating them:

"If you do not like to spend a lot of money, then you do not like shopping, and you do not like fashion."

Option K is the only option that fulfills the conditions of the contrapositive. All the other options are assumptions that are not necessarily supported by the contrapositive or the original statement.

ALL / SOME / NONE GAMES

All/Some/None games will provide you with a series of statements. Your job is to determine how these statements are connected.

For Example...

1. All squares are rectangles. Some rectangles are squares. No circles are rectangles.

Consider how the three statements above are connected. If all squares are rectangles but only some rectangles are squares, then it follows that not all rectangles are squares.

This means that the square is a sub-category of the rectangle.

Also, consider the third statement. When you take a look at the answer choices, remember that the circle is **NOT** a sub-category of the rectangle.

Now let's take a look at the question:

Based only on the information above, which of the following MUST be true?
A. Every rectangle is a square.
B. Some circles are considered squares.
C. Not all rectangles are squares.
D. There are no rectangles that are considered squares.
E. Most rectangles are squares.

Let's consider each answer choice carefully:

- Option A is incorrect because the question states that only "some" rectangles are squares.
- Option B is incorrect because the question states that "no circles" are squares.
- Option C is consistent with the statement "some rectangles are squares." Let's hold onto it.
- Option D is an untrue statement. "Some rectangles" are indeed squares.
- Option E is an assumption. "Some" does not equal "most."

Therefore, Option C is the best answer. It is consistent with the information provided and makes no assumptions about the question.

Always look for the answer choice that lines up most clearly with the statements provided.

ALL/SOME/NONE GAMES PRACTICE QUIZ

1. All zoos have monkeys. Some zoos have aquariums. All aquariums have clown-fish.

Based only on the information above, which of the following MUST be true?
A. All monkeys live in aquariums.
B. A zoo with an aquarium has clownfish.
C. Monkeys are more popular than aquariums.
D. Some zoos that do not have aquariums have seals.
E. Aquariums are mostly populated by clownfish.

2. All Vikings sailed in ships. No Vikings wore horned helmets. Some paintings show Vikings in ships wearing horned helmets.

Based only on the information above, which of the following MUST be true?
F. Vikings wore horned helmets when they weren't sailing.
G. All Vikings disliked horned helmets.
H. Some Vikings sailed in ships without wearing any helmets.
J. Painters exaggerate Viking fashion trends to make the art more exciting.
K. Paintings of Vikings wearing horned helmets are inaccurate.

3. All musicians practice. Some musicians improvise. All jazz musicians improvise. Improvisation does not require any practice.

Based only on the information above, which of the following MUST be true?
A. All musicians who improvise are jazz musicians.
B. No classical musicians improvise.
C. Musicians who improvise never practice.
D. Some musicians who improvise are jazz musicians.
E. It takes years of practice to be able to improvise.

4. All cats like treats. Some cats like baked beans. Some cats prefer baked beans when they're cold. Some cat owners consider baked beans a treat for their cat's.

Based only on the information above, which of the following MUST be true?

F. Some cats eat baked beans as a treat.

G. Some cats hate baked beans when they're hot.

H. Some cats prefer baked beans out of a can.

J. Some cat owners only feed their cat's baked beans as treats.

K. Some cat owners are manipulated by their cat's to feed them as many treats as possible.

ALL/SOME/NONE GAMES PRACTICE QUIZ SOLUTIONS

1. **B**   If some zoos have aquariums, and all aquariums have clownfish, then it follows that all zoos with aquariums have clownfish. This makes Option B the best answer. Option A is incorrect because the question never indicates that monkeys live in aquariums. Option C is an assumption that is not supported by the information provided. Option D can be ruled out because seals are never mentioned in the question. Option E is flawed because we don't know how many clownfish are typically kept in aquariums.

2. **K**   According to the question, no Vikings wore horned helmets. Therefore, a painting depicting Vikings with horned helmets would have to be considered inaccurate. Option K is correct. Option F is an assumption that is not supported by the information provided. Option G is incorrect because the question never mentions whether or not Vikings had any opinions about horned helmets. Option H can be ruled out because the question only states that Vikings did not wear "horned helmets." It does not suggest that Vikings didn't wear helmets at all. Option J might be true for some painters, but a motivation to make the art exciting is never mentioned or indicated in the question.

3. **D**   The question states that some musicians improvise and that all jazz musicians improvise. Thus jazz musicians belong to a subcategory of musicians who improvise. Although not all musicians who improvise are jazz musicians, we can conclude that some musicians who improvise must be jazz musicians. This makes Option D the best answer. Option A is incorrect because some musicians in other genres, such as rock, may also improvise. Option B is incorrect because the question never states anything about classical musicians. Option C can be ruled out because even though "improvisation does not require any practice," it is not correct to assume that musicians who improvise never practice. Option E is an opinion that is not supported by the information provided.

4. **F** If all cats like treats, some cats like baked beans, and some cat owners consider baked beans to be treats, then it follows that some cats eat baked beans as treats. This makes Option F the best answer. Option G is incorrect because the question never indicates how cats feel about hot baked beans. Option H can be ruled out because the question never states anything about cans. Option J might be true, but it is an assumption that is not supported by the information provided. Option K can be ruled out because the question never indicates that cats are capable of manipulating their owners.

DEDUCTION GAMES

Deduction games will present you with a short paragraph of conditions. You must assume that all the information provided is true, and you cannot assume any outside information.

Based on these conditions alone, you need to determine which answer **must** be true.

Look at each answer choice carefully. See if you can identify any flaws in the logic. The **LEAST** flawed answer choice is your **BEST** answer choice.

For Example...

1. All servers at Messy Joe's restaurant are required to spend time at the end of each shift doing side work. The manager is not required to do side work. Valerie is an employee at Messy Joe's who stayed at the end of her shift to do side work.

   Based only on the information above, which of the following MUST be true?
   A. Valerie is the manager.
   B. Valerie is a server.
   C. Valerie did side work voluntarily to prepare for the next day's work.
   D. Employees at Messy Joe's do side work only when it is required.
   E. If Valerie is the manager, then she did side work voluntarily.

According to the conditions, servers have to do side work but managers do not. The question tells us that Valerie did side work, but it does not tell us what her job is. This means that if she is the manager, she was not required to do side work but chose to do so anyway.

Let's look at each answer choice carefully in order to make our best guess:

- Option A is an assumption that is never stated in the question.
- Option B may seem likely since servers are required to do side work, but the question never indicates that only servers do side work. A manager might choose to do side work voluntarily.
- Option C might be true, but there is not enough information in the question to support it.
- Option D can be ruled out because we don't know what Valerie's job is. Therefore, we do not know whether she was required to do side work.
- Option E is the best answer. Valerie may or may not be the manager. If she is the manager, however, her side work was voluntary.

An answer choice is correct as long as an answer is 100% supported by the information provided. Eliminate any and all assumptions or answers that introduce outside information.

DEDUCTION GAMES PRACTICE QUIZ

1. Figure skaters in the Madison Figure Skating Championship are judged only on how many advanced jumps they complete. If a skater falls while attempting a jump, she will have one point deducted out of a possible six points for the routine. Sharon received a five out of six for her routine.

   Based only on the information above, which of the following MUST be true?
   A. Sharon either missed a jump or attempted too few jumps.
   B. Sharon missed at least one jump.
   C. Sharon missed exactly one jump.
   D. Sharon did not win the competition.
   E. Missing a jump is worse than not attempting it in the first place.

2. Dustin's cats are picky eaters who will not eat generic-brand cat food. They prefer the gourmet brand and will always eat it quickly. When Dustin gave the cats dinner last night, they finished it in one minute.

   Based only on the information above, which of the following MUST be true?
   F. Dustin gave the cats the gourmet brand.
   G. Both cats like the same food brands.
   H. Dustin gave the cats food from a brand other than the generic brand.
   J. The cats were exceptionally hungry.
   K. The cats' eating speeds depend on how much they like the food.

3. Everyone who majors in pre-law is planning to go to law school. Elle majored in biology, while her friend Adam majored in pre-law. One of them went to law school.

Based only on the information above, which of the following MUST be true?

A. If Elle went to law school, Adam changed his career plans.
B. Adam went to law school.
C. Elle went to law school.
D. Everyone who majors in pre-law succeeds in getting into law school.
E. If you don't major in pre-law, then you have no plans to go to law school

4. Evan is a photographer who feels that film photography is more expensive due to the cost of film, but digital photography is less artistically satisfying. He usually works with film.

Based only on the information above, which of the following MUST be true?

F. Evan's clients prefer film photography.
G. Evan does not care about expense at all.
H. Evan values saving money over artistry.
J. Evan can afford the added cost of buying film.
K. Evan is not a professional photographer.

DEDUCTION GAMES PRACTICE QUIZ SOLUTIONS

1. **A** A skater loses points for missing a jump. Since skaters are judged based on the number of completed jumps, it follows that they also lose points for attempting too few jumps. Since they are judged only on the number of completed jumps, these are the only two possible reasons Sharon could have lost a point. Therefore, Option A is the best answer. Option B is incorrect because Sharon may have completed all her jumps but done too few of them. Option C is incorrect because it might be possible to lose points for attempting too few jumps; therefore, this is not a statement that must be true. Option D is an assumption. Option E is an opinion that is not supported by the information provided.

2. **H** The question states that although the cats will not eat generic brand food, they did eat this particular brand of food. While we do not know what brand the food was, we can deduce that it was not a generic brand. This makes Option H the best answer. Option F is incorrect because although this option is possible, there may be other brands besides gourmet that the cats will eat. Option G is incorrect because although both cats like this particular food, they may not like all the same foods as each other. Option J can be ruled out because the question gives no indication as to how hungry the cats were. Option K is flawed because although we know that the cats eat the gourmet food quickly, there may be other foods that the cats eat just as quickly.

3. **A** Since all pre-law majors plan to go to law school; Adam must have planned to go. But we are told that either he or Elle went to law school—not both. Since it is entirely plausible that someone who didn't major in pre-law could still choose to go to law school, it follows that Elle could have gone. This makes Option A the best answer. Options B and C are incorrect because the question gives no indication that biology majors may not end up going to law school. Likewise, there is no indication that Adam didn't carry out his plan to attend law school. Option D can be ruled out because it does not necessarily follow that every pre-law major successfully manages to get into law school. Option E is an assumption that is not supported by the information provided.

4. **J** Since Evan chooses to use film despite its higher cost, he must be able to afford that cost. This makes Option J the best answer. Option F is incorrect because the question provides no indication as to whether Evan is a professional photographer, or, if so, what style his clients prefer. Option G is an extreme answer that may not necessarily be true. If he "usually" works with film, that means he occasionally uses digital. Therefore, it's possible that he may occasionally use digital to save money. Option H is incorrect because we are told that Evan has chosen a more artistically satisfying format over a cheaper one. Option K can be ruled out because Evan's choice of format gives us no clues as to whether he is a professional.

CONCLUSION GAMES

Conclusion games are similar to deduction games. Once again, you will be presented with a short paragraph of conditions.

Assume that all the information provided is true.

Based only on the conditions provided in the question, you need to determine which answer choice is the most valid conclusion.

For Example...

1. If a diner at Cheesecake Hut orders the Ultimate Pasta Bowl for an entrée, he will not be able to finish his cheesecake. Jiro went to Cheesecake Hut and finished his cheesecake.

    Based only on the information above, which of the following is a valid conclusion?

    A. Jiro did not order the Ultimate Pasta Bowl.
    B. Jiro ordered an entrée other than the Ultimate Pasta Bowl.
    C. The Ultimate Pasta Bowl contains more calories than any other entrée on the menu.
    D. If a diner orders an entrée other than the Ultimate Pasta Bowl, they will be able to finish their cheesecake.
    E. Jiro ate less overall than someone who had the Ultimate Pasta Bowl.

According to the question, ordering the Pasta Bowl is a circumstance that prevents any diner from finishing the cheesecake. If Jiro finished the cheesecake, he couldn't have ordered the Pasta Bowl.

Now let's look at each answer choice carefully:

- Option A seems to be a valid conclusion based on the information provided. Let's hold onto it!
- Option B is incorrect because the fact that Jiro did not have the Pasta Bowl does not mean he had a different entrée—he may have only ordered dessert.
- Option C can be ruled out because the calorie count is never mentioned.
- Option D is incorrect because we don't have enough information about the other entrées; some may actually be larger than the pasta bowl.
- Option E is incorrect because we don't have enough information about the other diners.

Therefore, the most valid conclusion is Option A.

REMEMBER: Don't assume anything outside of the information in the question. Eliminate any and all answers that introduce outside information.

CONCLUSION GAMES PRACTICE QUIZ

1. Jasmine is a real estate investor who bought an apartment complex in order to sell it for a profit. The expense of renovating the building was much higher than she expected. Jasmine ultimately sold the building for more than she bought it for.

    Which of the following pieces of additional information makes it possible to determine that Jasmine earned a profit on the building?
    A. The selling price was greater than the cost of the renovations.
    B. The difference between the buying and selling prices was greater than the cost of the renovations.
    C. The renovations added value to the building.
    D. Jasmine originally bought the building for a very low price.
    E. The cost of the renovations was tax-deductible.

2. Mark is unable to pay attention in class whenever he brings his computer. Mark is listening attentively in class.

    Based only on the information above, which of the following is a valid conclusion?
    F. Mark brought his computer.
    G. Mark is not using his computer in class.
    H. Mark's computer was not working today.
    J. Mark knows his grade will suffer if he does not pay attention.
    K. Cannot be determined from the information given.

3. Every philosopher in Boston is either an empiricist or a pragmatist. Dr. Mary Kurtz is a philosophy professor at Boston University.

    Which of the following pieces of additional information makes it possible to determine that Dr. Kurtz is an empiricist?
    A. Dr. Kurtz has written papers defending empiricism.
    B. Most philosophers in Boston are empiricists.
    C. Empiricism is much more common in Boston than elsewhere.
    D. No professor at Boston University is a pragmatist.
    E. It is impossible for the same person to be both an empiricist and a pragmatist.

4. Any employees who do not use all their vacation days by the end of the year will lose those vacation days for good.

Based only on the information above, which of the following is a valid conclusion?

F. If someone takes a vacation in December, he is doing so to use up his vacation days.

G. Employees will receive more vacation days in January.

H. An employee who takes a vacation day in January is not using a vacation day from the previous year.

J. The company created this policy to encourage people to use their vacation days.

K. If this policy did not exist, some employees would save up their vacation days instead of using them.

CONCLUSION GAMES PRACTICE QUIZ SOLUTIONS

1. **B** We already know that Jasmine spent money on the building, spent money on renovations and received money from the sale. In order to make a profit the amount she received must be greater than what she spent. This means that the selling price would have to be greater than the buying price and greater than the cost of the renovations. This makes Option B the correct answer. Option A is incorrect because this alone would not guarantee a profit, since Jasmine also spent money on buying the property. Although Option C might be true, there is not enough information to support this claim. Option D is irrelevant since we need to know whether she made a profit overall, not how much she spent on specific transactions. Option E has nothing to do with the question at all.

2. **G** The question indicates that Mark is distracted whenever he brings his computer to class. If he is listening attentively in class, then there is no way that he is using his computer. This makes Option G the best answer. Option F contradicts the question. Option H is incorrect because we don't have enough information about the state of his computer. Option J can be ruled out because his reasoning behind not using his computer is never mentioned.

3. **D** If every philosopher in Boston is either an empiricist or a pragmatist, and if no one at Boston University is a pragmatist, then Dr. Mary Kurtz must be an empiricist according to the logic of the question. Option A is incorrect; defending empiricism does not necessarily prove that you are an empiricist. Option B is flawed because of the word "most." That wouldn't prove that Dr. Mary Kurtz is an empiricist since she could still belong to a pragmatist minority. Option C is irrelevant to the question at hand. Option E might be true, but it would not necessarily result in the final conclusion.

4. **H**   The question tells us that any vacation days that are not used by the end of the year will not carry over into the new year. Therefore, someone who takes a vacation must be using vacation days they were issued during that year, not in the previous year. This makes Option H the best answer. None of the other options are supported by the information provided.

MATH GAMES

Math games should not be confused with math questions. Math games are simply Logical Reasoning questions that contain some math elements.

Usually, math games will ask you to add up the **greatest** or **least** number of items, depending on the conditions of the problem.

Like so many of the other Logical Reasoning question types, the best way to approach math games is to draw a diagram to keep the information organized.

For Example...

1. Gladys is a window washer who takes one minute to wash a window and one minute to travel between floors. The Eisenstein office building has ten floors. Eight of these floors have one window each, including the top floor. The other two floors have no windows.

    How many minutes will it take Gladys to finish cleaning the windows?
    A. 17
    B. 18
    C. 19
    D. 20
    E. 21

First of all, let's draw a diagram. Create a diagram with one row for each task and one column for each of the building's 10 floors:

Floor	Washing	Traveling
10		
9		
8		
7		
6		
5		
4		
3		
2		
1		

Mark an X for every minute Gladys spends on a given task. Since there are eight windows that Gladys needs to clean, the time spent washing the windows is eight minutes. Draw eight X's in the window-washing column.

Floor	Washing	Traveling
10	X	
9	X	
8	X	
7	X	
6	X	
5	X	
4	X	
3	X	
2		
1		

Next, draw in an X for each minute spent traveling between floors. Remember that since Gladys is starting on the first floor, she does not need to travel there. This means that she will be traveling up nine floors, giving us a total of nine minutes:

Floor	Washing	Traveling
10	X	X
9	X	X
8	X	X
7	X	X
6	X	X
5	X	X
4	X	X
3	X	X
2		X
1		

Add the total number of X's to reach the total time, which is 17 minutes.

Let's try another problem!

2. Throughout the year, Sheluyang works multiple jobs. He works as a copywriter for four months, a tutor for five months, and a graphic designer for four months. He never works more than two jobs at the same time.

What is the LEAST number of months Sheluyang could have worked all three jobs?

    F. 5
    G. 6
    H. 7
    J. 8
    K. 9

Start by creating a table. Divide the table into three rows, with each row representing one of Sheluyang's jobs. Next, divide the table into nine additional columns because nine is the greatest possible answer.

According to the problem, Sheluyang works as a tutor for five months, which means he spends more time tutoring than he does working as a copywriter or a graphic designer. Since the question is asking for the **LEAST** number of months, fill five X's into the first five columns of the Tutor row. Then, fill four X's into the first four columns of the Copywriter row:

MONTH	1	2	3	4	5	6	7	8	9
Copywriter	X	X	X	X					
Tutor	X	X	X	X	X				
Graphic Designer									

Don't forget that Sheluyang cannot work more than two jobs at a time. Therefore, he cannot start working as a graphic designer until Month 5. This means he can work as a graphic designer from Months 5 through 8:

MONTH	1	2	3	4	5	6	7	8	9
Copywriter	X	X	X	X					
Tutor	X	X	X	X	X				
Graphic Designer					X	X	X	X	

Once you've completed the diagram, count the number of columns with X's. According to this arrangement, the least number of months Sheluyang could work all three jobs is eight.

Remember: All you have to do on Math games is create a diagram, figure out the terms of the diagram, and keep a tally of X's or numbers until you reach your total.

MATH GAMES PRACTICE TEST

1. Giovanni is painting his garage. He must apply two coats of paint to each of the three walls. It takes one hour to paint a wall and two hours for a wall to dry.

    What is the LEAST number of hours it will take Giovanni to finish painting?
    A. 6
    B. 7
    C. 8
    D. 9
    E. 10

2. Dimitri's store is offering a deal: All five-dollar Zax candy bars will now cost three dollars, and all three-dollar Chox candy bars will cost two dollars. Jade bought three Zax bars and one Chox bar.

    How many dollars did Jade save?
    F. 5
    G. 6
    H. 7
    J. 8
    K. 9

3. To maximize his chances of getting into a good college, Abed plans to do extra-curricular activities in high school. He needs to spend four years in a language club, three years playing an instrument, two years on the debate team, and two consecutive years playing a sport. He must be on a sports team his senior year.

    What is the LEAST number of activities Abed can take during his sophomore year?
    A. 1
    B. 2
    C. 3
    D. 4
    E. 5

MATH GAMES PRACTICE TEST SOLUTIONS

1. **A** To solve this problem, draw a diagram with one column for each task Giovanni must complete. He needs to paint each of the three walls twice, which gives us a total of six tasks. Draw in an X for each hour it will take Giovanni to complete each task. Painting each wall takes one hour. However, you need to determine whether he will need to spend any time waiting for paint to dry. Note that since each wall takes two hours to dry, Wall 1 can be repainted by the time he is finished applying the first coat of paint to Wall 3. Wall 3 will be dry by Hour 5, which means he can repaint the third wall during Hour 6.

Hour 1	Hour 2	Hour 3	Hour 4	Hour 5	Hour 6
Paint Wall 1	Paint Wall 2	Paint Wall 3	Repaint Wall 1	Repaint Wall 2	Repaint Wall 3
X	X	X	X	X	X

This way, Giovanni does not need to waste any additional hours waiting for the paint to dry. The job will take him a total of six hours.

2. **H** Draw a diagram with one column for each individual candy bar Jade bought. In each column, draw an X for each dollar saved on that bar. Remember that she will save two dollars on each Zax bar and one dollar on each Chox bar. Therefore, you should draw two X's for each Zax column and one mark for each Chox column.

Zax	Zax	Zax	Chox
XX	XX	XX	X

Add up the total number of X's to determine the number of dollars saved. Jade saved a total of seven dollars.

3. **A** Draw a diagram with one column for each of Abed's four high school years. Create a row for each of his four activities. Draw an X for each activity that he must do in any given year. Draw four X's for Language club. We know that Abed must play a sport for two consecutive years including his senior year, so mark two X's in the Sports row for his junior and senior years. Also remember that the question is asking for the least number of activities Abed can do his sophomore year. This means that Abed can avoid playing an instrument his sophomore year by playing during his freshman, junior, and senior years. His years on the debate team do not have to be consecutive; mark two X's down for his freshman and junior or senior years.

	Freshman	Sophomore	Junior	Senior
Language club	X	X	X	X
Sports			X	X
Instrument	X		X	X
Debate	X		X	

Looking at the Sophomore column, we can see that he must do only one activity his sophomore year: Language club. Therefore, the least number of activities is one.

RECAP

This is a practice book. Use these passages to help you build your Logical Reasoning skills in order to raise your SHSAT results.

Use our "Question Type" guide to help determine which questions you excel at, and which questions you need to work on more.

Use the process of elimination on every single question. Don't eliminate answer choices in your head! Use your pencil to cross out flawed answers. The more you practice this skill, the quicker and easier it's going to be to make intelligent guesses as opposed to random guesses.

Check your work! After each practice test, look up the answers in the Solutions pages. Read the explanations carefully so you can better understand why you got a particular question wrong. It's okay to make mistakes, but learning from them will make you a stronger test-taker.

Time yourself! See how long it takes you to do an entire test. This will help you work on your time management skills. Remember: two and a half hours is not a long time to do every question on the SHSAT. Make sure you aren't rushing or dragging.

But most of all, **relax**. Believe in yourself. Test-taking is a skill, so improvement requires practice. It's no different from playing a musical instrument or a sport. The more you practice, the more your score will improve.

Good luck!

TEST ONE

Questions 1 and 2 refer to the following information.

In the code below, (1) each letter represents the same word in every sentence, (2) each word is always represented by only one letter, and (3) in any given sentence, the letters may or may not be presented in the same order as the words.

U	X	G	W	means
"John	likes	playing	soccer."	
E	L	U	X	means
"John	hates	playing	basketball."	
Y	U	K	M	means
"Mike	enjoys	playing	golf."	
U	G	F	Y	means
"Mike	likes	playing	tennis."	

1. Which word is represented by the letter X?

    A. playing

    B. soccer

    C. John

    D. hates

    E. basketball

2. Which letter represents the word "likes"?

    F. G

    G. Y

    H. U

    J. W

    K. Cannot be determined from the information given.

3. There are five cars participating in a cross-country race from New York City to Los Angeles. They will be ranked first through fifth based on how fast they make the trip.

    1) The red car finished before the green car and the yellow car.
    2) The blue car finished before the orange car but behind the yellow car.
    3) The orange car finished before the green car.

Which car finished last?
    A. red
    B. green
    C. orange
    D. blue
    E. yellow

4. Because Chase does not have a date to the prom, his girlfriend Mai must have broken up with him.

Based only on the information above, which of the following is a valid conclusion?
    F. If Mai refused to go to the prom, Chase would find another date.
    G. If Chase and Mai were still together, they still would not want to attend prom.
    H. If Chase and Mai were still together, they would definitely go to prom together.
    J. Chase and Mai have been having relationship problems for a long time.
    K. Mai would only break up with Chase if he refused to go to the prom with her.

5. It snowed heavily last night in Springfield. If the mayor declares a state of emergency, or the sidewalks become too icy to walk to class, Springfield University will close for the day. If the University stays open, all professors will hold class. The mayor did not declare a state of emergency, but no Springfield University students went to class today.

Based only on the information above, which of the following MUST be true?
   A. The students at Springfield University decided to skip class.
   B. If sidewalks were not icy, Springfield University students skipped class.
   C. The professors at Springfield University refused to teach due to the weather.
   D. Roads and sidewalks in Springfield were not badly affected.
   E. The students would have been in danger if they had gone to class.

6. Five girls on a basketball team are lined up according to height.

   1) Jenny is taller than Ruth and Marie.
   2) Ruth is taller than Liz, who is taller than Amy.
   3) Marie is taller than Ruth.

Which basketball player is in the third position?
   F. Jenny
   G. Ruth
   H. Marie
   J. Liz
   K. Amy

7. All students who have tutors want to improve their grades. Some students who improve their grades do not have tutors. No students improve their grades without studying.

Based only on the information above, which of the following MUST be true?

    A. A student forced to have a tutor does not want to improve his or her grades.

    B. Tutors ensure that students will improve their grades.

    C. All students who study will improve their grades.

    D. Some students who improve their grades have tutors.

    E. All students who do not have tutors do not want to improve their grades.

8. There are two new restaurants on President Street.

    1) The red restaurant has a small menu.

    2) The blue restaurant has recently been renovated.

    3) The fast food restaurant is more popular than the other restaurant.

    4) The gourmet restaurant has a large menu.

Based only on the information above, which of the following MUST be true?

    F. The red restaurant serves gourmet food.

    G. The blue restaurant is more popular than the red restaurant.

    H. The gourmet restaurant has recently been renovated.

    J. The fast food restaurant has a large menu.

    K. Cannot be determined from the information given.

9. If Sherry gets her hair cut, she gets her hair colored.

Based only on the information above, which of the following MUST be true?
   A. If Sherry does not get her hair cut, she does not get her hair colored.
   B. Whenever Sherry gets her hair colored, she also gets her hair cut.
   C. Only if Sherry gets her hair cut will she get her hair colored.
   D. If Sherry gets her hair cut, she will not get her hair colored.
   E. If Sherry does not get her hair colored, she did not get her hair cut.

10. At Macbeth University, families of graduating seniors receive tickets for the graduation ceremony. Those who are neither family members nor students can pay for a seat or sit on the lawn and watch the ceremony for free. Malachi watched the ceremony from the lawn.

Based only on the information above, which of the following MUST be true?
   F. Malachi is not a family member.
   G. Malachi could not get a ticket to graduation.
   H. Malachi did not pay for a ticket.
   J. Malachi is a graduating senior.
   K. Getting a seat is preferable to watching the ceremony from the lawn.

TEST ONE SOLUTIONS

1. **C** X appears in sentences 1 and 2 but not in sentences 3 or 4. The word "John" appears in sentences 1 and 2 but not in sentences 3 or 4. No other word appears only in sentences 1 and 2, so X must represent "John." Option A is incorrect because "playing" is in all 4 sentences. Option B is incorrect because "soccer" appears only in sentence 1. Option D is incorrect because "hates" appears only in sentence 2. Option E is incorrect because "basketball" appears only in sentence 2.

2. **F** The word "likes" appears in sentences 1 and 4 but does not appear in sentences 2 or 3. The letter G appears in sentences 1 and 4, but does not appear in sentences 2 or 3. No other letter appears only in sentences 1 and 4, so "likes" is represented by the letter G. Option G is incorrect because Y is in sentences 3 and 4. Option H is incorrect because U is in all four sentences. Option J is incorrect because W is only in sentence 1. Option K is incorrect because there is, in fact, enough information to determine that G means "likes."

3. **B** Rule 1 tells us that the red car finished before the green and yellow cars, but it does not say how the yellow and green cars finished:

$$\text{Red} \quad \rightarrow \quad \text{Green}$$
$$\text{Red} \quad \rightarrow \quad \text{Yellow}$$

Rule 2 tells us that the blue car finished between the yellow and the orange cars:

$$\text{Yellow/Orange} \quad \rightarrow \quad \text{Blue} \quad \rightarrow \quad \text{Orange/Yellow}$$

Combined with Rule 1 we have:

$$\text{Green}$$
$$\text{Red} \quad \rightarrow \quad \text{Yellow} \quad \rightarrow \quad \text{Blue} \quad \rightarrow \quad \text{Orange}$$

At this point, we do not know where Green finished compared to the other cars.

However, Rule 3 tells us that the green car finished after the orange car. Since we knew the orange car was behind the red, yellow, and blue cars, we can deduce that the green car finished last.

4. **H** The question states that Chase's lack of a prom date proves that his girl-friend Mai broke up with him. Therefore, if they had gone to prom together, they would still be in a relationship. This makes Option H the best answer. Option F is incorrect because it does not follow that Chase would find another date based on the information we have. Option G contradicts the question. Options J and K are incorrect because we do not have enough information about their relationship to reach these conclusions.

5. **B** According to the question, there are only two possible reasons for the University to be closed: a state of emergency or icy sidewalks. We know that a state of emergency was not declared, but we do not know whether or not the sidewalks were icy. If the sidewalks were not icy, the class would not have been canceled. Therefore, any student who was not there must have skipped class. Option B is the best answer.

Option A is not necessarily true because it does not address whether the sidewalks were icy. Option C can be ruled out because there is nothing mentioned in the question about the professors. Option D is incorrect because the fact that the mayor did not declare a state of emergency does not mean that roads were not badly affected. Option E is incorrect because students could have chosen to stay home even if the walk to class were not dangerous.

6. **G** Rule 1 tells us Jenny is taller than Ruth and Marie but does not tell us how Ruth compares to Marie:

> Ruth
>
> Jenny →
>
> Marie

Rule 2 tells us that Ruth is taller than Liz and that Liz is taller than Amy.

> Ruth → Liz → Amy

Rule 3 tells us that Marie is taller than Ruth. Now combine your diagrams to come up with the complete order:

> Jenny → Marie → Ruth → Liz → Amy

Ruth is the third tallest. Option G is the best answer.

7. **D** If all students who have tutors want to improve their grades, and some students who improve their grades do not have tutors, then it follows that some students with tutors will improve their grades. Thus Option D is correct. Option A can be ruled out because it contradicts the first statement in the question. Option B is an assumption that is not supported by the information provided. Option C is incorrect because studying is not a guarantee of improving grades. Option E can be ruled out because it contradicts the second statement in the question.

8. **H** Make a chart for the two restaurants: Red and Blue. Rule 1 tells you that the red restaurant has a small menu; mark it in your chart. Rule 2 tells you that the blue restaurant has recently been renovated; mark this in your chart as well.

Red	Blue
Small menu	Recently renovated

Rule 4 tells you that the gourmet restaurant has a large menu. Since the red restaurant has a small menu, that means the blue restaurant must have a large menu. We also now know that the blue restaurant is the gourmet restaurant, and the red restaurant is the fast food restaurant.

Red	Blue
Small menu	Recently renovated
Fast food	Large menu
	Gourmet

Rule 3 tells us that the fast food restaurant is more popular than the other restaurant which means that the red restaurant is more popular than the blue restaurant.

Red	Blue
Small menu	Recently renovated
Fast food	Large menu
Popular	Gourmet

Option F is incorrect because the blue restaurant is the restaurant that serves gourmet food, NOT the red restaurant. Option G is incorrect because the red restaurant is actually more popular than the blue restaurant. Option J is incorrect because the fast food restaurant has a small menu, NOT a large menu. Option H must be correct because the gourmet restaurant is the restaurant that was recently renovated; therefore it MUST be true.

9. **E**   Whenever you are dealing with an "If/Then" statement, remember that the contrapositive of the original statement is always correct. To form the contrapositive, one must reverse and negate the clauses. This gives you the following: "If Sherry does not get her hair colored, then she did not get her hair cut." Thus Option E is correct. Option A is incorrect because it is only the negative of the given statement, rather than the contrapositive. Option B reverses the clauses but neglects to negate the conditions. Option C is incorrect because it is extreme in introducing "only" as a condition. Option D can be ruled out because only the second clause is negated.

10. **H**   Since we know that anyone who wants to attend can watch the ceremony for free from the lawn, we can deduce that anyone who watched from the lawn did not pay for a ticket. This makes Option H the correct choice. Option F is possible, but there is not enough information to support it. Option G is incorrect because it is possible that Malachi received a ticket but chose to sit on the lawn. Option J is incorrect because if Malachi were graduating, he would likely participate in the ceremony rather than just watch it. Option K is an opinion that is not supported by the information provided.

TEST TWO

1. There are five race cars of different colors taking part in a race: red, blue, yellow, green, and purple.

   1) The green car finished the race before the red car.
   2) The yellow car finished directly behind the red one.
   3) The red car came in second place.
   4) The car that finished last was not red, green, or blue.

   In which place did the blue car finish?
   A. first
   B. second
   C. third
   D. fourth
   E. fifth

2. Annabelle, Brady, Cory, Declan, and Enoch each take turns picking movies for a weekly movie night. There have been five movie nights so far. They chose a drama, a comedy, a documentary, an experimental film, and a horror film.

   1) The documentary is shown third.
   2) Three movies are shown in between Brady's and Cory's selections.
   3) The comedy is shown the week before Cory's selection.
   4) The experimental film is shown after the drama.
   5) The horror film was chosen by Annabelle and was shown the week after Brady's selection.
   6) Declan did not choose the comedy.

   Which movie did Declan choose?
   F. comedy
   G. documentary
   H. horror
   J. drama
   K. experimental

3. If Betty plays the piano, then Sam will sing. If Sam sings, then the dog will howl.

Based only on the information above, which of the following MUST be true?
   A. If Sam is singing, then Betty must be playing the piano.
   B. If the dog is howling, then Sam must be singing.
   C. If the dog is howling, then Betty must be playing the piano.
   D. If Betty is not playing the piano, then the dog is not howling.
   E. If the dog is not howling, then Betty is not playing the piano.

4. Some dancers study ballet. All professional dancers study their craft for many years. Some dancers who study dance have fun.

Based only on the information above, which of the following MUST be true?
   F. If you are not having fun, then you are not dancing.
   G. Only professional dancers study dance for many years.
   H. Some dancers who study ballet have fun.
   J. All ballet dancers have fun.
   K. If you study your craft for many years, then you must be a dancer.

Questions 5 and 6 refer to the following information.

In the code below, (1) each letter always represents the same word, (2) each word is always represented by only one letter, and (3) the position of a letter is never the same as that of the word it represents.

Z	A	B	0	means
"Jarret	likes	watching	basketball."	
J	K	0	G	means
"Mary	likes	making	cookies."	
X	R	D	0	means
"Bob	likes	making	birdhouses."	
B	E	0	A	means
"Karen	likes	watching	TV."	

5. Which letter represents the word "basketball"?
  A. A
  B. B
  C. K
  D. Z
  E. Cannot be determined from the information given.

6. Which word is represented by the letter A?
  F. watching
  G. likes
  H. basketball
  J. Karen
  K. Cannot be determined from the information given.

7. Greg is on time for work if he gets the 9:00 train. Bob has time to buy bagels for the office if Greg is on time for work.

   Based only on the information above, which of the following MUST be true?
   A. If Bob does not have time to buy bagels for the office, then Greg did not get the 9:00 train.
   B. If Greg is not on time for work, Bob will not buy bagels for the office.
   C. If Greg is not on the 9:00 train, Bob will not buy bagels for the office.
   D. If Greg does not get the 9:00 train, then Greg is not on time for work.
   E. If Greg is not on time for work, then Bob will not buy bagels for the office.

8. Amber takes four yearly vacations within four years. She visits India, Switzerland, Jamaica, and Peru. On each vacation, she stays at a different type of accommodation: a hostel, a hotel, a cabin, and a guest house.

   1) She visits India first.
   2) She visits Switzerland two years before she stays in the hostel.
   3) She stays in the hotel two years after staying at the guest house.
   4) The hostel is located in Peru.

   In which country does Amber stay in a cabin?
   F. India
   G. Switzerland
   H. Jamaica
   J. Peru
   K. Cannot be determined from the information given.

9. The Andersons have twelve bottles in their refrigerator. This includes six bottles of water, one bottle of milk, and two bottles of orange juice. Each of the other bottles contains a different type of soda. How many total different beverage types do they have in their refrigerator?

    A. 4
    B. 5
    C. 6
    D. 7
    E. 8

10. Because Destiny does not have any cats or dogs, she must be allergic to them.

Which of the following pieces of additional information makes it possible to determine that she is allergic to cats and dogs?

    F. Destiny loves animals and would like to have pets.
    G. Cats and dogs are a common cause of allergies.
    H. Cats and dogs are the only animals that cause allergies.
    J. Allergies are the only thing stopping Destiny from having a cat or dog.
    K. Cats are more popular than dogs.

TEST TWO SOLUTIONS

1. **D** As you decode the order of the race cars, focus on one condition at a time. The third condition tells us that the red car finished the race in second place. The green car then must have finished the race in first place because the first condition tells us that the green car finished the race before the red car. The yellow car must have finished the race in third place because the second condition states that the yellow car finished directly behind the red one. The fourth condition tells us that the car in last place was not red, green, or blue—which means it was the purple car. This leaves the blue car, which must have been in fourth place.

Green → Red → Yellow → Blue → Purple

2. **G** Start by creating a table with one row for the people's names and one row for the movie genres. Rule 1 tells you that the documentary is shown third, so write that in first. Rule 2 then states that three movies are shown in between Brady's and Cory's selections. This means that these movies must be in Positions 1 and 5 although you cannot yet determine which is which. Looking at Rule 3 tells you that Cory's selection must be shown in Week 5 since another movie is shown before hers. Thus, the comedy is in Position 4.

Brady				Cory
		documentary	comedy	

Since you now know that Brady's selection is in Week 1, you can use the information from Rule 5: The horror film was chosen by Annabelle and was shown the week after Brady's selection in Week 2. There are now only two movies whose positions are unknown. Rule 4 tells you that the experimental film is shown after the drama, so you can write them in for Weeks 1 and 5. Finally, we know that Declan did not choose the comedy. Enoch chose the comedy, and Declan chose the documentary, which is the second answer choice.

Brady	Annabelle	Declan	Enoch	Cory
drama	horror	documentary	comedy	experimental

3. **E** First, combine the sentences to create one "If/Then" statement:

"If Betty plays the piano, then Sam will sing, and the dog will howl."

Next, form the contrapositive in order to figure out which answer choice must be true. The contrapositive is formed by reversing and negating the clauses. This is reflected in Option E, which is correct. Options A, B, and C simply reverse the clauses without making then negative. Option D negates the clauses without reversing them.

4. **H** The third statement tells us that some dancers who study dance have fun. Thus some dancers who study ballet must also be having fun. This makes Option H correct. All the other answer choices are assumptions and generalizations that are not supported by the information provided.

5. **D** The word "basketball" only appears in the first sentence. The only answer choice that only appears in the first sentence is Z. Since Z is not in the same position as "basketball," Z must represent this word. K only appears in the second sentence. Options A and B can also be ruled out because they both appear in the fourth sentence.

6. **F** The word "watching" appears in sentences 1 and 4. The only two letters to appear only in these sentences are A and B. We know A cannot represent "likes" because the third rule for this question type states that "the position of a letter is never the same as that of the word it represents." Therefore, A must represent the word "watching."

7. **A** First, combine the two statements:

"If Greg gets the 9:00 train, then Greg is on time for work and Bob has time to buy bagels for the office."

The contrapositive is formed by reversing and negating both clauses. The only answer choice that fulfills the conditions of the contrapositive is Option A. All the other options can be ruled out because they represent assumptions that are not supported by the information provided.

8. **G**   Draw a four-column table with one row for the countries and one for the different types of accommodations. Rule 1 tells you that Amber visits India in year 1, so write that in first. Next, look at Rule 2. She visits Switzerland two years before she stays in the hostel. That means that there is one year between the Switzerland trip and the hostel trip. Since India is already in the Year 1 position, you can deduce that she visited Switzerland in Year 2 and the hostel in year 4. Rule 4 tells you that she stayed in the hotel two years after staying at the guest house. In other words, there is one vacation in between the hotel and guest house trip. Since she stays at the hostel in Year 4, the guest house and hotel trips took place in Years 1 and 3:

India	Switzerland		
guest house		hotel	hostel

The only remaining type of accommodation, the cabin, can be assigned to Year 2. Since we now know that the hostel appears fourth in the sequence, we can use the information from Rule 4: The hostel is located in Peru. Finally, the one remaining country, Jamaica, can be assigned to Year 3.

India	Switzerland	Jamaica	Peru
guest house	cabin	hotel	hostel

The question is asking for the country in which Amber stayed in the cabin. Option G is correct.

9. **C** Draw a chart with one column for every drink type. Start with the 6 waters, 2 orange juices, and 1 milk. Write the number of bottles into the chart in order to keep track of how many are left. Water, orange juice, and milk account for 9 of the bottles. According to the premise, there are 12 bottles in total. If the rest of the fridge contains different types of soda, and each soda type is only represented by one bottle, then there must be 3 types of soda left.

Water	Orange juice	Milk	Soda 1	Soda 2	Soda 3
6	2	1	1	1	1

The question is asking for the number of different beverage types. There are 6 in total, which means Option C is correct.

10. **J** In order for Destiny's lack of pets to prove that she is allergic, we would have to be certain that allergies are the only thing that could prevent her from having pets. This makes Option J correct. Option F does not, by itself, support the conclusion because even if she wants pets, some other cause could prevent her from having them. Option G is incorrect because, while this information makes it more likely that Destiny suffers from allergies, it is not necessarily true. Option H is incorrect because whether or not other animals cause allergies is irrelevant to determining Destiny's reasons for not having pets. Option K is irrelevant because the question tells us that Destiny does not have either cats or dogs.

———— TEST THREE

1. Four cars made in four separate countries—Japan, Germany, the United States, and Sweden—are parked in a row on a street in that order. Their colors are blue, black, green, and red.

   1) The blue car is Japanese.
   2) The red car is parked to the left of the black car.
   3) There are two cars in between the green car and the blue car.

   What color is the American car?
   A. black
   B. blue
   C. green
   D. red
   E. Cannot be determined from the information given.

2. All English teachers are good writers. Some writers write every day. No math teacher writes every day.

   Based only on the information above, which of the following MUST be true?
   F. All English teachers write every day.
   G. No math teacher is a good writer.
   H. If someone writes every day, then he must be an English teacher.
   J. If you are not a good writer, then you must be a math teacher.
   K. If you are not a good writer, then you are not an English teacher.

3. At his most recent job, Rashan coded software using several computer pro-
    gramming languages. He coded in Python for three years, Ruby for three years,
    and PHP for three years. He never coded more than two computer program-
    ming languages during the same year. In his last year on the job, Rashan only
    coded in Ruby?

    **What is the least number of years Rashan could have coded for his
    job?**
    A. 4
    B. 5
    C. 6
    D. 7
    E. 8

4. John is shopping for the cheapest tie he can find.

    1) The red tie is cheaper than the blue tie but more expensive than the
        purple tie.
    2) The green tie is more expensive than the yellow tie.
    3) The yellow tie is cheaper than the purple tie.

    Which tie does John buy?
    F. red
    G. blue
    H. purple
    J. green
    K. yellow

5. Yara, Zelda, Xavier, and Quesha are in line in the cafeteria. The students are in 9th, 10th, 11th, and 12th grade, respectively.

1) Zelda is a 9th grader.
2) The 11th grader is on the far left.
3) The student second from the right is neither a 9th nor a 10th grader.
4) There are no students to the right of Yara.
5) The 9th grader is to the left of the 10th grader.

What grade is Yara in?
    A. 9th
    B. 10th
    C. 11th
    D. 12th
    E. Cannot be determined from the information given.

Questions 6 and 7 refer to the following information.

In the code below, (1) each letter represents the same word in every sentence, (2) each word is always represented by only one letter, and (3) in any given sentence, the letters may or may not be presented in the same order as the words.

V	**K**	**M**	**E**	means
"Bill	eats	fried	shrimp."	
P	**V**	**E**	**T**	means
"Dawn	eats	fried	shrimp."	
P	**G**	**L**	**K**	means
"Bill	likes	steamed	mussels."	
U	**L**	**T**	**M**	means
"Dawn	likes	fried	clams."	

6. Which letter represents the word "eats"?

    F. V
    G. L
    H. T
    J. K
    K. M

7. Which word is represented by the letter K?

    A. Bill
    B. eats
    C. shrimp
    D. dawn
    E. fried

8. Maurice applied for two jobs: A higher-paying but more stressful job and a lower-paying but more enjoyable job. Maurice ended up taking the higher-paying job.

Based only on the information above, which of the following MUST be true?

    F. Maurice was offered both jobs.

    G. Maurice was offered the higher-paying job.

    H. Maurice values higher pay over a stress-free work environment.

    J. Higher-paying jobs are more stressful than lower-paying jobs.

    K. Maurice is happy with the pay rate at his new job.

9. Josh, Luke, Hannah, Catie, and Drew are ordering at a restaurant. Their orders include fajitas, chimichangas, tacos, burritos, and enchiladas.

1) The person having enchiladas orders first.
2) Drew places his order three spots after the person who ordered chimichangas.
3) Catie ordered immediately after the person who had the burrito.
4) Josh ordered before Luke but after Hanna.
5) Catie did not have the fajitas.

Which meal did Luke have?
A. burritos
B. chimichangas
C. tacos
D. enchiladas
E. fajitas

10. Jenny has five dresses. She hangs up the dresses in order of preference.

1) She likes the brown dress the least.
2) She likes the red dress more than the green dress.
3) She likes the pink dress less than the red dress but more than the yellow dress.

Which dress is Jenny's second favorite dress?
F. red dress
G. green dress
H. pink dress
J. yellow dress
K. Cannot be determined from the information given.

TEST THREE SOLUTIONS

1. **A** Create a chart with one column for each car and one row for each of the two attributes. Fill in the top row with the order of the cars given in the question: starting with the Japanese car first, followed by the German car, then the American car, and finally by the Swedish car. Now look at the rules to determine the color of each car. The clearest piece of information is that the Japanese car is blue according to Rule 1, so write that in first. According to Rule 3, there are two cars between the green car and the blue car. If the Japanese car is blue and there are two cars between it and the green car, then the Swedish car must be green. We are left with the red and black cars. According to Rule 2, the red car is to the left of the black car. This means that the German car must be red, and the American car must be black. Therefore, Option A must be correct.

Japanese	German	American	Swedish
Blue	Red	Black	Green

2. **K** Option K is correct because the question states that all English teachers are good writers. Thus if you are not a good writer, you cannot be an English teacher. Option F is false because the question does not give enough detailed information to conclude that all English teachers write every day. Option G can be ruled out because writing every day does not mean you are a good writer. Moreover, you could write less often, yet still, be a good writer. Option H is incorrect because the question never establishes that all good writers write every day. Option J is false because it is not necessarily true that someone who is not a good writer must be a math teacher. Some math teachers may be good writers, and a non-writer could belong to some other profession.

3. **B** Draw and label a diagram like the one below. The question does not state the order in which Rashan coded each computer programming language. It does, however, say that Rashan only coded in Ruby during his last year at his job. As such, we will save this information for later. While we can pick any language to begin with, we will start with Python for this example. Under Year 1, mark an X in the row for Python. Because the question states that Rashan coded Python for three years, we can also mark X's under Year 2 and Year 3.

Year	1	2	3	4	5	6	7	8	9
Python	X	X	X						
Ruby									
PHP									

Now let's look at the condition. The condition states that Rashan never coded more than two computer programming languages during the same year. As such, we can pick PHP as the next computer programming language, and mark X's under Year 1 and Year 2 in the row for PHP.

Year	1	2	3	4	5	6	7	8	9
Python	X	X	X						
Ruby									
PHP	X	X							

Under Year 3, mark an X in the row for Ruby. We do this rather than mark an X for PHP under Year 3, because if we marked an X in the PHP row under Year 3, we would then need to mark X's for the Ruby row in Year 4, Year 5, and Year 6, for a total of 6 years. This, however, would be incorrect because the question is asking for the least number of years. Instead, we will mark X's in the row for Ruby under Year 3, Year 4, and Year 5.

Year	1	2	3	4	5	6	7	8	9
Python	X	X	X						
Ruby			X	X	X				
PHP	X	X							

We can now add an X in the row for PHP under Year 4. Mapping out Rashan's programming languages in this way ensures that we are meeting the condition that he code no more than two languages during the same year, and that he code only in the Ruby computer programming language in his final year on the job.

Year	1	2	3	4	5	6	7	8	9
Python	X	X	X						
Ruby			X	X	X				
PHP	X	X		X					

The least number of years Rashan could have coded for his job is five years. Option B is correct.

4. **K** Rule 1 tells us that the red tie is cheaper than the blue tie but more expensive than the purple tie:

Blue → Red → Purple

Rule 2 tells us that the green tie is more expensive than the yellow tie:

Green → Yellow

Rule 3 tells us that the yellow tie is cheaper than the purple tie, which we already know is cheaper than the blue and red ties based on Rule 1:

Blue → Red → Purple → Yellow

Although we don't know where the green tie stands in the complete sequence, we do know that it is more expensive than the yellow tie. This means that the yellow tie must be the cheapest tie. Therefore, John bought the yellow tie.

5. **B** Draw a chart with one row for the student names and one row for the grade levels. Start with the information you can enter into the chart. Rule 2 states that the 11th grader is on the far left, so fill that in first. Since Rule 2 states that the student second from the left is not a 9th or 10th grader; the student second from the right must be the 12th grader. Since the 9th grader is to the left of the 10th grader according to Rule 5, we can place them in the second and fourth slots, respectively.

11th	9th	12th	10th

The next task is to match the names to the grade years. Rule 1 states that Zelda is in 9th grade. Rule 4 states that there are no students to the right of Yara. This means that Yara is in last place. Note that the question does not give you enough information to place Quesha and Xavier in their correct slots. However, you do not need this information to answer the question. Yara is in 10th grade, which is Option B.

Quesha/ Xavier	Zelda	Xavier/ Quesha	Yara
11th	9th	12th	10th

6. **F** The word "eats" appears in sentences 1 and 2 only. The letter V is the only letter that appears only in sentences 1 and 2. No other letters or words appear only in sentences 1 and 2. The letter E also appears, but it is not given as an option in the answer choices.

7. **A** The letter K appears in sentences 1 and 3. The word "Bill" also only appears in sentences 1 and 3. K and "Bill" are the only letter and word that appear in both sentences 1 and 3. Option G is incorrect because "eats" appears in sentences 1 and 2. Option H is incorrect because "shrimp" appears in sentences 1 and 2. Option J is incorrect because "Dawn" appears in sentences 2 and 4. Option K is incorrect because "fried" appears in sentences 1 and 4.

8. **G** We are told in the question that Maurice applied for two jobs. Since he ultimately accepted the higher-paying job, he must have been offered that job. Thus Option G is correct. Options F and H are incorrect because there is not enough information to determine whether he was even offered the lower-paying but more enjoyable job. Option J might be true, but there is not enough information in the question to support it. Option K is an assumption that is not supported by the information provided.

9. **A** Create a five-column diagram with one row for the names and one for the food items. Rule 1 tells you that enchiladas were ordered first, so start by writing that in. Since enchiladas were ordered first, chimichangas must have been ordered second because Rule 2 tells us that Drew placed his order three spots after the person who ordered chimichangas. Rule 3 states that Catie ordered immediately after the person who had the burrito. Since there are only two columns unoccupied, these two items can be placed in Columns 3 and 4.

			Catie	**Drew**
enchiladas	chimichangas	burrito		

Rule 4 tells us that Josh ordered before Luke but after Hanna. This allows us to place them in Columns 1, 2, and 3. Finally, you are told that Catie did not have the fajitas. There is only one other person who could have ordered the fajitas: Drew. This means Catie ordered the tacos.

Hannah	**Josh**	**Luke**	**Catie**	**Drew**
enchiladas	chimichangas	burritos	tacos	fajitas

The question is asking for the meal that Luke ordered. Option A is correct.

10. **K** Rule 1 states that the brown dress is Jenny's least favorite, so we know this dress will be in last place.

Rule 2 states that she likes the red dress more than the green dress. Now we can work out part of the sequence. Place the dresses in order from left to right in order of most preferred to least preferred:

$$\text{Red} \quad \rightarrow \quad \text{Green} \quad \rightarrow \quad \text{Brown}$$

Rule 3 states that Jenny likes the pink dress less than the red dress but more than the yellow dress:

$$\text{Red} \quad \rightarrow \quad \text{Pink} \quad \rightarrow \quad \text{Yellow} \quad \rightarrow \quad \text{Brown}$$

However, the rules do not provide the relationship between the green and pink dresses, or the green and yellow dresses. All we know is that red is her favorite, and brown is her least favorite. Since we cannot work out the complete sequence, the dress she likes the third best cannot be determined from the information given.

———————— TEST FOUR

1. Five wrestlers participate in a weigh-in for a tournament. They are lined up according to their weights, from heaviest to lightest.

   1) Mike weighs less than John but more than Steve.
   2) Steve weighs more than Luke but less than Roger.
   3) Roger weighs more than John.

   In which position is Steve?
   A. first
   B. second
   C. third
   D. fourth
   E. Cannot be determined from the information given.

2. Sheetal painted flowers on her wall. She painted seven yellow flowers, four green flowers, two red flowers, and five blue flowers. She could only paint a maximum of three flowers each day before she became too tired to paint any longer. With the exceptions of the first and last days, she never painted flowers of different colors on the same day.

   What is the least number of days Sheetal could have painted all the flowers?
   F. 6
   G. 7
   H. 8
   J. 9
   K. 10

3. Luke spots a man on a park bench taking a sandwich from a bag that reads "Greens Restaurant." Luke concludes that the sandwich must be vegetarian.

Which of the following pieces of additional information makes it possible to determine that the sandwich is vegetarian?
  A. Most people in Luke's city are vegetarian.
  B. People who eat meat rarely eat at Greens Restaurant.
  C. Greens Restaurant offers vegetarian food.
  D. Greens Restaurant serves all different types of sandwich.
  E. Greens Restaurant only serves vegetarian food.

4. A large cheese pizza from Bellagio's costs $10. Josiah ordered food at Bellagio's Pizza. The total cost of his order was $20.

Based only on the information above, which of the following MUST be true?
  F. Josiah ordered more than one pizza.
  G. Josiah ordered toppings on his pizza.
  H. Josiah ordered multiple pizzas, each with extra toppings.
  J. Josiah did not order just a large cheese pizza.
  K. Josiah ordered two large cheese pizzas.

5. If a defendant pleads guilty to burglary, he will receive a prison sentence. Talbot was tried for burglary but did not receive a prison sentence.

Based only on the information above, which of the following is a valid conclusion?
  A. Talbot is innocent.
  B. Pleading guilty to burglary is a foolish act.
  C. Any defendant who pleads not guilty to burglary will not receive prison time.
  D. Talbot was found not guilty.
  E. Talbot pled not guilty.

6. Any server at the Red Lion who works a double shift will be the first to be let off work in the evening. Ash worked at the Red Lion in the evening and was the first to get off work.

Based only on the information above, which of the following MUST be true?

F. Ash worked a double shift.
G. Ash did not work a double shift.
H. Either Ash worked a double shift, or no one did.
J. Working a double shift is difficult and tiring.
K. No one worked a double shift.

7. Barry always goes to the circus if there are clowns in the show. Pat always takes her nephew to the circus if there are clowns in the show.

Based only on the information above, which of the following MUST be true?

A. If Pat does not take her nephew to the circus, then Barry does not go to the circus.
B. If Barry goes to the circus, then Pat takes her nephew to the circus.
C. If Pat does not take her nephew to the circus, then Barry goes to the circus.
D. Barry does not go to the circus if Pat does not go to the circus.
E. Both Barry and Pat love clowns.

Questions 8 and 9 refer to the following information.

In the code below, (1) each letter represents the same word in every sentence, (2) each word is always represented by only one letter, and (3) in any given sentence, the letters may or may not be presented in the same order as the words.

B	**X**	**T**	**L**	means
"Doug	drinks	cold	coffee."	
M	**V**	**T**	**B**	means
"Doug	drinks	hot	tea."	
T	**P**	**L**	**K**	means
"Mark	drinks	cold	milk."	
T	**P**	**M**	**X**	means
"Mark	drinks	hot	coffee."	

8. Which word is represented by the letter P?

    F. Mark
    G. drinks
    H. cold
    J. hot
    K. coffee

9. Which letter represents the word "milk"?

    A. P
    B. L
    C. K
    D. T
    E. M

10. Five boys ran a race around a mile-long track. At the end of the race, there were no ties.

     1) John finished before Ben but behind Mark and Seth.

     2) Seth finished before Ralph, who finished before Ben.

     3) Mark finished before Seth.

Which boy finished last?

    F. John

    G. Ben

    H. Mark

    J. Seth

    K. Cannot be determined from the information given.

TEST FOUR SOLUTIONS

1. **D** Rule 1 states that Mike's weight is between those of John and Steve:

John → Mike → Steve

Rule 2 tells us that Steve's weight is between those of Roger and Luke. While this rule doesn't reference John or Mike, it does reference, Steve. Since we know that Luke is lighter than Steve, we can work out two possible sequences:

Roger → Steve → Luke

OR

John → Mike → Steve → Luke

Rule 3 states that Roger weighs more than John. This puts Roger at the front of our list based on Rule 2, which tells us that Steve is the fourth heaviest. The final sequence is as follows:

Roger → John → Mike → Steve → Luke

2. **F** Draw a diagram like the one below. The problem tells us that on the first day, Sheetal painted flowers in up to two different colors. If she could only paint three flowers throughout the day, she could have painted the 2 red flowers and 1 yellow flower on Day 1. On Days 2 and 3, she could have painted the 6 remaining yellow flowers; 3 yellow flowers each day. Then, on Day 4, she could have painted 3 green flowers and 3 blue flowers on Day 5. On Day 6, the 1 remaining green flower and the 2 remaining blue flowers could have been painted. The least number of days to paint all the flowers is 6 days. Option F is the correct answer:

Days

	1	2	3	4	5	6	7
Yellow	1	3	3				
Green				3		1	
Red	2						
Blue					3	2	

3. **E** We are told that Luke sees a sandwich from Greens Restaurant and concludes that it must be vegetarian. This is a valid conclusion only if this restaurant does not serve non-vegetarian food; this is represented by Option E. Option A is incorrect because it does not necessarily prove that the sandwich is vegetarian. Option B is incorrect because this statement bears no relation to whether Greens Restaurant only serves vegetarian food. Option C is incorrect because Greens could offer both vegetarian and non-vegetarian food. Option D makes the conclusion less likely because it implies that the man's sandwich could contain anything.

4. **J** The question tells us the cost of a large cheese pizza, but not the cost of toppings or of other pizza sizes. Since Josiah spent more than the cost of a single large cheese pizza, all we can deduce is that he ordered something other than, or in addition to, a large cheese pizza. This makes Option J the best option. Option F is incorrect because we do not know the cost of the toppings. Option G is incorrect because he may have ordered multiple plain pizzas. Option H is possible, but it is not necessarily true. Option K is possible based on the cost of a large cheese pizza, but it is not a valid conclusion without knowing the cost of the other menu items.

5. **E** The question states that anyone who pleads guilty will receive prison time. Thus if someone is tried for burglary but does not receive prison time, they must have pled not guilty. This makes Option E correct. Option A is incorrect because Talbot could be innocent or he could be guilty yet not in prison, as there was not enough evidence to convict him. Option B is an opinion that is not supported by the information provided. Option C is incorrect because the fact that everyone who pleads guilty will receive a prison sentence does NOT mean that everyone who pleads not guilty will not receive a prison sentence. Option D is incorrect because Talbot could have either been found not guilty or he could have been found guilty but received a punishment that did not involve prison time.

6. **H** If Ash worked a double shift, he would be the first to leave. But if no one worked a double shift, someone who did not work a double shift would be the first to leave. Since Ash was first to leave work, it follows that either he worked a double shift or no one did. This makes Option H correct. Option A is incorrect because it is possible that on some days no one works a double shift. In that case, Ash could be first to leave without working a double shift. Option B is incorrect because the fact that he was first to leave makes it more likely that he worked a double shift. Option J is possible but is not supported by the information provided. Option K is incorrect because the question does not indicate whether any server worked a double shift.

7. **A**   First, combine the two statements to form one "If/Then" clause:

"Barry goes to the circus, and Pat takes her nephew to the circus if there are clowns in the show."

Option A is the contrapositive of the merged given statements; in order to form the contrapositive, one must switch the clauses and make them both negative. Thus Option A is correct. Option B is incorrect because Barry and Pat are not necessarily related. Option C only negates the clauses without reversing their order and therefore is not definitely true. Option D does not switch the clauses. Option E is an assumption that is not supported by the information provided.

8. **F**   The letter P appears only in sentences 3 and 4. The word "Mark" also appears only in sentences 3 and 4. "Mark" and the letter P are the only word and letter, respectively, that are exclusive to sentences 3 and 4. Option G is incorrect because "drinks" appears in all four sentences. Option H is incorrect because "cold" appears in sentences 1 and 3. Option J is incorrect because "hot" appears in sentences 2 and 4. Option K is incorrect because "coffee" appears in sentences 1 and 4.

9. **C**   The word "milk" appears only in sentence 3. The letter "K" appears only in sentence 3. No other letter appears only in sentence 3. Thus Option C is correct.

10. **G**   Draw out each rule one by one. Once all three rules are drawn out, you can determine the correct sequence.

Rule 1 tells us that John finished before Ben but lost to Mark and Seth. This rule does not tell us in what order Mark and Seth finished, so this is all we know right now:

$$\begin{matrix} \text{Mark} \\ \text{Seth} \end{matrix} \rightarrow \text{John} \rightarrow \text{Ben}$$

Rule 2 tells us that Seth finished before Ralph, who finished before Ben:

$$\text{Seth} \rightarrow \text{Ralph} \rightarrow \text{Ben}$$

Rule 3 tells us that Mark beat Seth. Now we can determine part of the sequence:

$$\text{Mark} \rightarrow \text{Seth} \rightarrow \text{John} \rightarrow \text{Ben}$$

However, we don't know where exactly Ralph finished. All we know is that he finished between Seth and Ben. Thus the best way we can rank the participants is as follows:

$$\text{Mark} \rightarrow \text{Seth} \rightarrow \begin{matrix} \text{John} \\ \text{Ralph} \end{matrix} \rightarrow \text{Ben}$$

Since the question is asking for who finished last, we can conclude that it must have been Ben.

TEST FIVE

1. Jimmy is shopping for a new car. He has narrowed his choices down to five and decides to rank them from cheapest to most expensive.

   1) The red car is cheaper than the green, yellow, and blue cars.
   2) The yellow car is more expensive than the blue car but cheaper than the green car.
   3) The brown car is cheaper than the red car.

   Which car is the second cheapest?
   A. red
   B. green
   C. yellow
   D. blue
   E. Cannot be determined from the information given.

2. Four diners are eating breakfast around a square table: Bartholomew, Cady, Devon, and Ethel. Two of the diners are eating bacon and eggs, one is eating pancakes, and one is eating a breakfast burrito.

   1) Cady is sitting next to Ethel.
   2) Bartholomew ordered the burrito.
   3) The two people eating bacon and eggs are sitting next to each other.
   4) Cady is across from someone eating bacon and eggs.

   Which of the diners ordered the pancakes?
   F. Bartholomew
   G. Cady
   H. Devon
   J. Ethel
   K. Cannot be determined from the information given.

Questions 3 and 4 refer to the following information.

In the code below, (1) each letter represents the same word in every sentence, (2) each word is always represented by only one letter, and (3) in any given sentence, the letters may or may not be presented in the same order as the words.

K	X	N	J	G	means
"Jill	watches	movies	on	TV."	
J	T	N	F	X	means
"John	watches	sports	on	TV."	
R	T	G	N	D	means
"John	records	movies	on	cable."	
D	N	K	X	F	means
"Jill	watches	sports	on	cable."	
D	N	S	T	R	means
"John	records	westerns	on	cable."	

3. Which letter represents the word "sports"?

    A. R
    B. X
    C. T
    D. F
    E. N

4. Which word is represented by the letter G?

    F. John
    G. records
    H. movies
    J. cable
    K. on

5. Damacio, a college student, must take three more courses in mathematics, four more courses in physics, and two more courses in biology in order to graduate. He can take no more than two courses at a time, and he can not take biology and mathematics courses simultaneously. What is the least number of semesters he will need to complete in order to graduate?

    A. 3
    B. 4
    C. 5
    D. 6
    E. 7

6. All students must submit their Standardized College Potential Test scores (SCPTs) to be considered for acceptance at State University. Valerie got into State University.

Based only on the information above, which of the following is a valid conclusion?
    F. Valerie took the SCPTs.
    G. Valerie did not take the SCPTs.
    H. Valerie received a good score on the SCPTs.
    J. If a student receives good SCPT scores, she will be accepted at State University.
    K. If a student is not accepted at State University, she did not submit her SCPT scores.

7. If Greg goes to the college library, he will never borrow more than three books in one trip.

Based only on the information above, which of the following MUST be true?
   A. If Greg has five books on his shelf, then he did not go to the college library.
   B. If Greg borrowed three books, then he must have gone to the college library.
   C. If Greg borrowed more than three books, then he must have gone to the college library.
   D. If Greg borrowed two books, then he went to the college library.
   E. If Greg borrowed six books in one trip, then he did not go to the college library.

8. Dr. Bahrani treats five patients in one day: Amber, Becky, Clint, Dale, and Earl. They are treated for a burn, strep throat, anemia, a sprain, and insomnia, respectively.

   1) Clint is treated after the patient with anemia.
   2) Amber is treated after the patient with strep but before the patient with a burn.
   3) Dale is not treated last.
   4) Becky is treated before Dale.
   5) The insomnia patient is treated before the anemia patient.

For which ailment is Earl treated?
   F. burn
   G. strep throat
   H. anemia
   J. sprain
   K. insomnia

9. Jacob is playing with building blocks. He stacks them up with the biggest block on the bottom and the smallest block on top.

1) The yellow block is smaller than the green block but bigger than the orange block.
2) The green block is bigger than the brown block but smaller than the red block.
3) The brown block is bigger than the orange block.

Which block is on the top?
    A. yellow
    B. green
    C. orange
    D. red
    E. Cannot be determined from the information given.

10. Professor Greenwood gave each student in her class a "late paper coupon." The coupon allows a student to turn in one of the five assigned papers late without a penalty. Five of her fifteen students turned in their final papers late.

Based only on the information above, which of the following MUST be true?
    F. Five students used their coupons on their final papers.
    G. Between one and five students used their coupons on their final papers.
    H. The other ten students used their coupons earlier in the semester.
    J. All five students received penalties on their final papers.
    K. No more than five students used their coupons on their final papers.

TEST FIVE SOLUTIONS

1. **A** Draw a diagram for each rule in order to carefully work out the correct sequence.

   Rule 1 tells us that the red car is cheaper than the green, yellow, and blue cars, but it does not tell us how the green, yellow, and blue cars compare to one another. So all we know so far is that the red car is either the first or second cheapest.

   Rule 2 tells us the relationships between the green, yellow, and blue cars. Now, we can combine the first two rules to determine how all four cars rank according to price:

   $$Red \rightarrow Blue \rightarrow Yellow \rightarrow Green$$

   Rule 3 tells us that the brown car is cheaper than the red car. We now have the full sequence:

   $$Brown \rightarrow Red \rightarrow Blue \rightarrow Yellow \rightarrow Green$$

   Therefore, the second cheapest car is red.

2. **G** To diagram this problem, draw two intersecting lines. The ends of each spoke will represent each diner. Next, since Rule 1 states that Cady is next to Ethel, write those names in. Note that it does not matter whether Cady is to Ethel's right or left—your diagram may be a mirror-image version of the one shown below. Next, look for another piece of information you can write in the diagram. Cady is across from someone eating bacon and eggs.

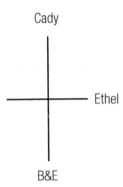

Since Rule 2 states that the two people eating bacon and eggs are next to each other, the other person who ordered eggs is either Ethel or the un-identified person opposite her. But note that Rule 2 tells you Bartholomew ordered the burrito. Bartholomew must be the person opposite Ethel, which means that Ethel also ordered eggs. There is now only one unassigned meal: the pancakes. Cady must have ordered the pancakes. The only unas-signed person, Devon, must be across from Cady. Option G is correct.

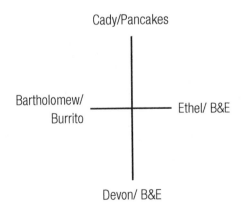

3. **D** The word "sports" appears in sentences 2 and 4 only. The letter F appears in sentences 2 and 4 only. No other word or letter is exclusive to sentences 2 and 4.

4. **H** The letter G appears only in sentences 1 and 3. The word "movies" appears only in sentences 1 and 3. All the other options appear in 3 or all 5 of the sentences, not just in sentences 1 and 3.

5. **C** To solve this problem, make a chart with ten columns and four rows and add the column and row headings.

Semester

	1	2	3	4	5	6	7	8	9
Math									
Physics									
Biology									

The first sentence tells us that Damacio must take three mathematics courses, four physics courses, and two biology courses for a total of nine additional courses in order to graduate. The second sentence tells us that he can only take two courses at a time, and he can not take biology and mathematics course at the same time. Mark three semesters for math and four semesters for physics.

Semester

	1	2	3	4	5	6	7	8	9
Math	X	X	X						
Physics	X	X	X	X					
Biology									

Starting at semester 4, mark two semesters for biology.

Semester

	1	2	3	4	5	6	7	8	9
Math	X	X	X						
Physics	X	X	X	X					
Biology				X	X				

Our completed chart shows that Damacio has taken no more than two courses each semester and that he has not taken math and biology courses in the same semester. When we count the number of semesters with marks in them, we see that the least number of semesters Damacio will need to complete in order to graduate is 5 semesters. Option C is the correct answer.

6. **F**   The question tells us that submitting SCPT scores is necessary for being accepted at State University. This tells us that anyone accepted to State University must have submitted his or her SCPTs. Since Valerie was accepted, she must have taken the SCPTs. Thus Option F is correct. Option G is incorrect because if Valerie did not take the SCPTs, she would not have been eligible to be accepted at State University. Option H is never mentioned in the question. Option J is incorrect because the fact that SCPT scores are considered does not mean that good scores guarantee acceptance. Option K is incorrect because there could be many other reasons that a student could be rejected.

7. **E** Form the contrapositive by switching the "if" and "then" clauses and negating them. You will produce a new "if" clause:

"If Greg borrows more than three books in one trip, then he did not go to the library."

This coincides with Option E. Option A is an assumption that is not necessarily true. Options B, C, and D, reverse the clauses but do not negate them. Pay attention to how you form the contrapositive, not just to the number of books, as the contrapositive is the only statement other than the original that we can rely on.

8. **F** Create a table with one row for the patients and one row for the medical conditions. Next, look for the first piece of information that you can clearly enter into the table. Rule 1 tells us that Clint is treated after the patient with anemia:

	Clint					
anemia						

Rule 2 tells us that Amber is treated after the patient with strep but before the patient with a burn. Because we do not yet know how Amber or the conditions relate to Clint, we will simply enter the information next to Clint and then adjust as necessary as the rest of the information becomes clear to us:

	Clint		**Amber**			
anemia		strep throat		burn		

Rule 5 states that the insomnia patient is treated before the anemia patient. This means that we will need to adjust our table to add the insomnia condition before the anemia condition:

		Clint		Amber		
insomnia	anemia		strep throat		burn	

Looking back at Rule 2, we see that Amber was treated for an unknown ailment between the patients with strep throat and burn, respectively. The only ailment missing from our chart is the sprain, which must be Amber's ailment. If Amber has the sprain, then Clint must have strep throat:

		Clint	Amber			
insomnia	anemia	strep throat	sprain	burn		

Looking at Rule 3, we see that Dale is not treated last, which means he must be treated either first or second. Rule 4, however, states that Becky is treated before Dale, thereby indicating that Dale is treated second, Becky is treated first, and Earl is treated last.

Becky	Dale	Clint	Amber	Earl		
insomnia	anemia	strep throat	sprain	burn		

The question is asking for Earl's ailment, which is a burn. Option F is the correct answer.

9. **C** Rule 1 tells us that the yellow block is between the green and orange blocks:

> Orange
> Yellow
> Green

Rule 2 tells us that the green block is between the red and brown blocks, but we do not know how the brown block compares to the yellow or orange blocks:

> Brown
> Green
> Red

We can combine Rules 1 and 2 to determine how four of the blocks relate:

> Orange
> Yellow   Brown
> Green
> Red

We cannot include the brown block in the stack with the other four since we only know its relationship to the green block. Rule 3 confirms that the brown block is bigger than the orange block.

> Orange
> Yellow   Brown
> Green
> Red

Even though we cannot determine exactly where the brown block ranks, we can still determine that the orange block is the smallest block and must be on the top.

10. **K**   Since the coupons allow the students to turn in their papers late without penalty, a student turning in a paper on time would not need to use it. Therefore, if five students turned their papers in late, up to five of them—but no more than five—may have used their coupons to avoid penalties. This makes Option K correct. Option F is possible but is not necessarily true. Option G is incorrect because it is possible that all the students in the class used their coupons earlier in the semester. Option H is incorrect because it is possible that some of the ten students who turned in their papers on time never used their coupons. Option J is incorrect because, since some or all of the students may have used the coupon, we cannot determine whether they received penalties.

——————— TEST SIX

1. Henri's Restaurant is serving dessert. There are five couples and five individual diners eating in the restaurant. Three couples decided to share dessert. The remaining couples ordered individuals desserts. All the individual diners ordered dessert.

   How many total desserts does the restaurant serve?
      A. 10
      B. 11
      C. 12
      D. 14
      E. 15

Questions 2 and 3 refer to the following information.

In the code below, (1) each letter represents the same word in every sentence, (2) each word is always represented by only one letter, and (3) in any given sentence, the letters may or may not be presented in the same order as the words.

M	W	C	P	V	means
"Blue	birds	swim	in	lakes."	
T	P	W	H	L	means
"Green	fish	swim	in	rivers."	
C	X	D	O	T	means
"Green	birds	dive	under	water."	
B	V	H	W	M	means
"Blue	fish	jump	in	lakes."	
C	B	J	L	N	means
"Yellow	birds	jump	over	rivers."	

2. Which word represents the letter M?

    F. blue
    G. jump
    H. lakes
    J. birds
    K. Cannot be determined from the information given.

3. Which letter represents the word "fish"?

    A. W
    B. T
    C. H
    D. L
    E. Cannot be determined from the information given.

4. All parents love their children. Some parents spoil their children. All parents who spoil their children do not discipline their children.

   Based only on the information above, which of the following MUST be true?
   F. Some parents who discipline their children spoil their children.
   G. All parents who do not discipline their children spoil their children.
   H. All parents who discipline their children do not spoil their children.
   J. No good parents spoil their children.
   K. Spoiling your children is bad parenting.

5. Betty decided that she wanted to create a list of her five favorite foods. She ranked her five favorite foods from first through fifth.

   1) Betty likes pizza more than steak but less than chocolate.
   2) Betty likes steak more than hamburgers.
   3) Betty likes turkey more than steak.

   Which food is Betty's favorite?
   A. pizza
   B. steak
   C. chocolate
   D. turkey
   E. Cannot be determined from the information given.

6. Cameron and Maria ride their bicycles together on their way to school every morning.

    1) One of the bicycles is green.
    2) The blue bicycle does not have a bell.
    3) The mountain bike does not have a basket.
    4) The touring bike is blue and has a basket.

Based only on the information above, which of the following MUST be true?
    F. The green bicycle has a bell.
    G. The blue bicycle has no basket.
    H. The green bicycle has a basket.
    J. The green bicycle is a touring bike.
    K. Cannot be determined from the information given.

7. Four people are camping in a line alongside a river: Luke, Frances, Robin, and Gillian. They are camping in a red tent, a blue tent, an RV, and a motorhome, respectively.

    1) Robin is to the right of Frances and to the left of the camper in the RV.
    2) Gillian is on the far left in the motor home.
    3) Luke is on the far right.
    4) Luke is not next to the camper in the red tent.

Which camper is in the blue tent?
    A. Gillian
    B. Frances
    C. Robin
    D. Luke
    E. Cannot be determined from the information given.

8. Because Morrigen was not at the concert on Saturday night, she must have been unable to get off work.

    Which of the following pieces of additional information makes it possible to determine that Morrigen was unable to get off work?

    F. Morrigen wanted to go to the concert.
    G. Morrigen has a demanding work schedule and usually works on Saturdays.
    H. Morrigen tried to get off work on Saturday night.
    J. Morrigen would definitely have gone to the concert had she gotten off work.
    K. Morrigen did not have a ticket to the concert.

9. For two nights, Lamar played jazz trumpet at a Brooklyn coffee shop.

1) Lamar played on Monday night and Tuesday night.
2) Lamar wore a red jacket and black shoes during the Tuesday show.
3) On the night he wore a green jacket, he also wore blue shoes with no sunglasses.
4) Lamar wore a flat cap on the same night he wore black shoes.

Based only on the information above, which of the following COULD be true?

A. Lamar did not wear a flat cap during the Tuesday show.
B. Lamar did not wear a flat cap during the Monday show.
C. Lamar wore sunglasses during the Monday show.
D. Lamar wore a red jacket during the Monday show.
E. Lamar wore a green jacket during the Tuesday show.

10. If pigs can fly, then cats can bark.

Based only on the information above, which of the following MUST be true?

    F. If pigs cannot fly, then cats cannot bark.

    G. If cats can bark, then pigs can fly.

    H. When pigs can fly, then all cats can bark.

    J. If cats cannot bark, then pigs cannot fly.

    K. Cats can only bark when pigs can fly.

TEST SIX SOLUTIONS

1. **C** The question states that there are fifteen diners in total. To find out how many desserts were ordered, draw a diagram with one column for each diner. You should have fifteen columns in total. Next, draw an X in the column for each diner who ordered dessert. If three couples shared dessert, then at least six people ate dessert. Fill X's into every other column until you have skipped 3 columns. Since every remaining diner after the first three couples ordered their own desserts, fill X's into all the other columns after Column 6:

1	2	3	4	5	6	7	8	9	10	11	12	13	14	15
X		X		X		X	X	X	X	X	X	X	X	X

Finally, add up all the X's in your diagram to determine how many desserts were served. The correct answer is 12.

2. **K** The letter M appears in sentences 1 and 4 only. But there are two words that appear exclusively in sentences 1 and 4: "blue" and "lakes." Because M could represent either of these two words, it cannot be determined from the information given.

3. **C** The word "fish" appears in sentences 2 and 4 only. The letter H also appears only in sentences 2 and 4. The letter W is in sentences 2 and 4, but it also appears in sentence 1. Option A is incorrect because W appears in sentence 1 as well as sentences 2 and 4. Option B is incorrect because the letter T appears in sentences 2 and 3. Option D is incorrect because the letter L appears in sentences 2 and 5. Option E is incorrect because there is indeed enough information to determine that "fish" is represented by the letter H.

4. **H** The question distinguishes between parents who spoil their children and parents who discipline their children. According to the question, if a parent disciplines his or her children, this parent does not spoil his or her children. This makes Option H correct. All the other options are assumptions and generalizations that are not supported by the information provided.

5. **E** Rule 1 tells us that Betty ranked pizza between chocolate and steak.

$$\text{Chocolate} \quad \rightarrow \quad \text{Pizza} \quad \rightarrow \quad \text{Steak}$$

Rule 2 tells us that Betty ranked steak above hamburgers. Combine this piece of information with Rule 1 for part of the sequence:

$$\text{Chocolate} \quad \rightarrow \quad \text{Pizza} \quad \rightarrow \quad \text{Steak} \quad \rightarrow \quad \text{Hamburgers}$$

Rule 3 tells us only that Betty likes turkey more than steak. This rule does not tell us how turkey compares to chocolate or pizza. We know that turkey is at least her third favorite food, but it could rank higher than pizza or chocolate. The question is asking what Betty's favorite food is, but it cannot be determined from the information given.

6. **K** Make a chart for the two bicycles. Carefully fill in each characteristic of the two bicycles to keep the information organized. We know that the blue bicycle has no bell based on Rule 2, however, we do not know whether the green bicycle has a bell as it is not explicitly stated in Rule 2, nor is it implied in any of the other rules. As such, we cannot assume that the green bicycle has a bell. According to Rule 4, the blue bicycle is a touring bike. This bike also has a basket. Rule 3 tells us that the green bicycle is a mountain bike and does not have a basket:

Blue Bicycle	Green Bicycle
Basket	No Basket
No Bell	
Touring Bike	Mountain Bike

With the chart completely filled in, we can answer the question. Option K is the only statement that is supported by the information provided.

7. **C** Draw a chart with four columns and two rows: one for camper name and one for shelter type. Since Rule 1 tells us that Frances is to the left of both Robin and the RV camper, she must be in either Position 1 or Position 2. To figure out which is correct, look at Rule 2. Gillian is in Position 1, so Frances must be in position 2, which is directly to Gillian's right. Rule 3 allows us to write in Luke as the camper in the RV. Rule 2 also tells us that Gillian is in the motorhome.

Gillian	Frances	Robin	Luke
motorhome			RV

Only the two tents must now be filled in. Since Luke is not next to the red tent, he is next to the blue tent. The red tent belongs to Frances.

Gillian	Frances	Robin	Luke
motorhome	Red tent	Blue tent	RV

8. **J** The fact that Morrigen was not at the concert does not prove she had to go to work unless her job was the only thing that could have caused her to miss the concert. This makes Option J correct. Option F is incorrect because even if Morrigen wanted to go, some other factor could have prevented her from attending the concert. Option G is incorrect because, while it suggests that Morrigen was scheduled to work Saturday, it tells us nothing about whether other factors could have made her miss the concert. Option H is incorrect because it tells us nothing about whether she succeeded in getting off work. Option K does not support the conclusion because if Morrigen did not have a ticket, her work schedule is irrelevant.

9. **B** Draw a diagram to help you keep the information organized. Rule 2 states that Lamar wore a red jacket and black shoes during the Tuesday show, so fill that in first. Rule 3 tells us that he wore a green jacket and blue shoes, with no sunglasses, during Monday's show. Rule 4 says that Lamar wore a flat cap on the same night he wore black shoes which was during Tuesday's show, so fill that in. Your completed chart should look something like this:

Monday	Tuesday
green jacket	red jacket
blue shoes	black shoes
no sunglasses	flat cap

Options A, C, D, and E are all incorrect because none of them are true. This leaves Option B as the only answer choice that **COULD** be true. None of the rules conclusively indicate whether or not Lamar wore a flat cap during Monday's show. Option B is the only answer choice that accurately reflects a possible circumstance being true.

10. **J** Form the contrapositive of the given statement by reversing and negating the clauses. The contrapositive is always true, and is reflected in Option J. Option F makes the clauses negative without reversing them, while Option G reverses the clauses without negating them. Option H is an extreme statement that is not supported by the information provided. Option K does not negate the two clauses.

———— TEST SEVEN

1. Jessica is shopping for work clothes. She needs a total of four outfits. Each day she must wear a top and a skirt. As long as she does not repeat a combination, Jessica can reuse individual articles of clothing in putting together her four outfits.

    What is the LEAST number of items Jessica could buy?
    - A. 4
    - B. 5
    - C. 6
    - D. 7
    - E. 8

2. At senior prom, Janet wants to dance with the second shortest boy in her class.

    1) Joseph is shorter than Mark and Lance.
    2) Lance is taller than Mark and Roger.
    3) Roger is taller than Timmy, who is taller than Mark.

    With whom does Janet want to dance?
    - F. Lance
    - G. Mark
    - H. Joseph
    - J. Roger
    - K. Timmy

3. If Mary goes to the nightclub, then she goes dancing. If she goes dancing, then she will be in a good mood.

Based only on the information above, which of the following MUST be true?

A. If Mary does not go to the nightclub, then she will not be in a good mood.

B. If Mary goes dancing, then she will be in a good mood because she went to the nightclub.

C. If Mary is happy, then she has gone dancing.

D. If Mary is in a good mood, then she has gone to the nightclub.

E. If Mary is not in a good mood, then she has not gone to the nightclub.

4. Alfred and Bertha are jurors on a trial. They agree that whoever gave the victim a ride home on the date of the crime must be guilty. Alfred thinks the defendant is innocent, while Bertha thinks the defendant is guilty.

Based only on the information above, which of the following MUST be true?

F. The defendant gave the victim a ride home from work.

G. Alfred and Bertha disagree on the significance of giving the victim a ride from work.

H. Alfred and Bertha disagree on the importance of evidence.

J. Alfred and Bertha disagree on whether the defendant gave the victim a ride.

K. The trial will result in a hung jury because the jurors cannot agree on a verdict.

Questions 5 and 6 refer to the following information.

In the code below, (1) each letter represents the same word in every sentence, (2) each word is always represented by only one letter, and (3) in any given sentence, the letters may or may not be presented in the same order as the words.

R	E	T	N	X	means
"Blue	skies	mean	nice	weather."	
D	T	N	K	R	means
"Black	skies	mean	bad	weather."	
M	Y	D	R	G	means
"People	run	from	bad	weather."	
H	X	V	T	C	means
"John	rests	under	blue	skies."	
K	C	H	T	F	means
"John	works	under	black	skies."	

5. Which word is represented by the letter R?

    A. blue
    B. weather
    C. bad
    D. skies
    E. mean

6. Which letter represents the word "skies"?

    F. T
    G. C
    H. V
    J. X
    K. H

7. Because Josh moved out of his apartment after living there for only three months, he must have broken the terms of his lease.

Which of the following pieces of information makes it possible to determine that Josh broke his lease?

A. Most leases require tenants to stay for twelve months or more.

B. Josh had a lease that required him to stay for more than three months.

C. Anyone who breaks a lease is vulnerable to receiving a penalty.

D. Leaving an apartment after only three months is inconvenient for landlords.

E. When Josh moved out, his landlord charged him a fee.

8. All music has a specific rhythm. Some music is syncopated. Some music has an even beat. Music that is syncopated can also have an even beat.

Based only on the information above, which of the following MUST be true?

F. Music rhythms are either syncopated or even.

G. No music can have more than one type of rhythm.

H. Syncopation is more interesting than even rhythm.

J. Even beats are better than syncopation.

K. Rhythm is a component of all music.

9. Ray, Dave, Mick, and Pete went to a music shop on Record Store Day. Each bought exactly one record: a jazz record, a blues record, a rock record, and a rap record.

1) Ray did not buy the rock or the rap record.
2) Either Mick or Dave bought the jazz record.
3) Pete bought the rap record.

Who bought the jazz record?

A. Ray
B. Dave
C. Mick
D. Pete
E. Cannot be determined from the information given.

10. Five kinds of cheese are lined up on a cheese tray: Gouda, Brie, cheddar, goat cheese, and Emmenthaler. Each cheese costs a different amount of money.

1) Brie is the second most expensive cheese and is positioned on the far left.
2) Emmenthaler is directly to the right of the first most expensive cheese and three spaces to the right of the fifth most expensive cheese.
3) The third most expensive cheese is to the left of the most expensive cheese.
4) Gouda is between Brie and goat cheese.

Which is the most expensive cheese?

F. Gouda
G. Brie
H. cheddar
J. Emmenthaler
K. goat cheese

TEST SEVEN SOLUTIONS

1. **A**   Since we are looking for the least number of items Jessica could buy, start with the smallest answer choice, which is 4. Draw a diagram with one column for each of the two tops Jessica buys and one row for each of the two skirts. The number of X's in the diagram will be the number of resulting outfits:

	Top 1	**Top 2**
Skirt 1	X	X
Skirt 2	X	X

There are 4 X's in the above diagram. This means that she could reuse each top and each skirt twice without repeating the combinations:

Top 1/Skirt 1   Top 1/Skirt 2   Top 2/Skirt 1   Top 2/Skirt 2

Therefore, the least number of items she could buy is 4.

2. **G**   Rule 1 states that Joseph is shorter than Mark and Lance, but it doesn't tell us the relationship between Mark and Lance:

> Mark
>
>   Joseph
>
>   Lance

Rule 2 tells us that Lance is taller than Mark and Roger. We do not know the relationship between Mark and Roger. Draw out a diagram using only the information you know for sure:

> Lance → Mark → Joseph
>
>
>
> Roger

Rule 3 tells us how Roger compares to Mark by telling us that Roger is taller than Timmy and that Timmy is taller than Mark. Finally, we can put all the rules together for the complete sequence:

Lance → Roger → Timmy → Mark → Joseph

Therefore, Janet wants to dance with Mark.

3. **E** First, combine the two statements:

"If Mary goes to the nightclub, then she goes dancing, and she will be in a good mood."

Option A makes the "If/Then" clauses negative. This does not form the contrapositive because the clauses must also be reversed. Option B is not necessarily correct because other circumstances besides dancing could make her happy. Options C and D only reverse the clauses without negating them. Option E correctly forms the contrapositive and therefore must be true. It is the only answer choice that cannot be argued against.

4. **J** The question tells us that the jurors agree on the significance of the ride as a sign of guilt. Since they disagree on whether the defendant is guilty, but each thinks whoever gave the ride is guilty, they must disagree about whether the defendant gave out the ride. Option F is incorrect because the question gives us no clues as to whether Alfred or Bertha is correct. Option G cannot be true because the question tells us they agree. Option H is never mentioned in the question. Option K is incorrect because although they do not agree now, they may be able to reach an agreement before the trial is over.

5. **B** R appears in the first three sentences only. The word "weather" appears in these three sentences only. No other letters or words appear exclusively in sentences 1, 2, and 3.

6. **F**   "Skies" appears in sentences 1, 2, 4, and 5. The letter T also appears in sentences 1, 2, 4 and 5. Neither "skies" nor the letter T appears in sentence 3. Option G is incorrect because the letter C only appears in sentences 4 and 5. Option H is incorrect because the letter V only appears in sentence 4. Option J can be ruled out because the letter X appears in sentences 1 and 4 but not sentences 2 and 5. Option K is incorrect because H only appears in sentence 4.

7. **B**   Knowing that Josh moved out after three months does not, by itself, tell us that he broke his lease. We would have to know that he signed a lease requiring him to stay for some period of time greater than three months. This makes Option B correct. Option A does not mention anything about Josh's agreement with his landlord. Option C is incorrect because the question never mentions anything about a penalty. Option D is incorrect because it does not prove that all landlords require longer tenancy. Option E does not support the conclusion because we do not know what the fee was for.

8. **K**   The first line of the question tells us that all music has rhythm. This means that rhythm must be a component in all music. Thus Option K is correct. All the other options are assumptions and opinions that are not supported by the information provided.

9. **E**   Draw a diagram like the one below. First, fill in the fact that Pete bought the rap record according to Rule 3. Next, take a look at Rules 1 and 2. If Ray did not buy the rock record, and either Mick or Dave bought the jazz record, then Ray must have bought the blues record. However, there is not enough information to determine whether Mick or Dave bought the jazz record, so the correct answer is Option E:

Ray	Dave	Mick	Pete
Blues	Rock/Jazz	Jazz/Rock	Rap

10. **H** Draw a chart with five columns and two rows (for cheese name and price ranking). First, write in the information from Rule 1: Brie is on the far left and is ranked second in price. Next, look at Rule 2. Rule 2 states that Emmenthaler is three spaces to the right of the fifth most expensive cheese. This means there are two kinds of cheese between Emmenthaler and the fifth most expensive cheese. Since Brie is on the far left and is the second most expensive, the fifth most expensive cheese must be in Position 2. Rule 2 also states that the Emmenthaler cheese is directly to the right of the first most expensive cheese. This means that the first most expensive cheese must be in Position 4:

Brie				Emmenthaler
second	fifth		first	

Next, Rule 3 states that the third most expensive cheese is to the left of the most expensive cheese. There is only one remaining space to the left, so you can write in the positions of the cheeses ranked third and fourth. Finally, according to Rule 4, Gouda is between Brie and goat cheese. There is only one remaining space left next to Brie, so you can write in the positions of Gouda and goat cheese. The only remaining cheese, Cheddar, can now be placed on the chart:

Brie	Gouda	Goat cheese	Cheddar	Emmenthaler
second	fifth	third	first	fourth

The question is asking for the most expensive cheese. Option H is correct.

——— TEST EIGHT

1. Andy, Bertrand, Corinna, and Dermot have placed their lunches in a row from left to right on the refrigerator shelf. The lunches include a sandwich, a salad, a casserole, and a pork chop.

   1) Dermot's lunch is on the far left.
   2) Andy's lunch is two spaces to the right of the sandwich.
   3) The pork chop is to the left of the sandwich.
   4) Corinna's lunch is to the right of Bertrand's and is not the salad.

   Which lunch did Corinna bring?
   A. sandwich
   B. salad
   C. casserole
   D. salad
   E. Cannot be determined from the information given.

2. All New Yorkers consider New York State their home. Some New Yorkers live in New York City. Some New Yorkers were born in New York City.

   Based only on the information above, which of the following must be true?
   F. Some New Yorkers who live in New York City were not born there.
   G. All New Yorkers were born in New York City.
   H. Only New Yorkers who live in New York City consider New York State their home.
   J. New Yorkers never leave New York State.
   K. Cannot be determined from the information given.

3. If Leo does not want to listen to rock and roll music, then he does not want to listen to heavy metal.

    Based only on the information above, which of the following MUST be true?
    A. If Leo does not want to listen to heavy metal, then he does not want to listen to rock and roll music.
    B. If Leo wants to listen to rock and roll music, then he wants to listen to heavy metal.
    C. If Leo wants to listen to heavy metal, then he wants to listen to rock and roll music.
    D. If Leo does not want to listen to rock and roll and heavy metal music, then he does not like music.
    E. If Leo does not like rock and roll music, then he likes heavy metal.

4. Marie paid for her groceries in cash. She must have gone to the ATM recently.

    Based only on the information above, which of the following is a valid conclusion?
    F. Marie works at a job that does not pay in cash.
    G. Marie frequently stops at the ATM.
    H. Marie bought her groceries at a store that only takes cash.
    J. Marie did not receive any tips at work.
    K. The ATM is Marie's only possible cash source.

5. Advanced Chemistry is a required course for pre-med majors. Students must pass Introductory Chemistry to take Advanced Chemistry. Marissa took Introductory Chemistry but did not take Advanced Chemistry.

Based only on the information above, which of the following MUST be true?
   A. Marissa failed Introductory Chemistry.
   B. Marissa either failed Introductory Chemistry or passed it but is not a pre-med major.
   C. Marissa passed Introductory Chemistry.
   D. Only pre-med students take Advanced Chemistry.
   E. Marissa must either re-take Introductory Chemistry or change her major.

6. Oswald and Oliver are twin brothers. Their parents purchase one birthday cake for each child.

   1) Oliver's cake is vanilla-flavored, and Oswald's cake is strawberry-flavored.
   2) The strawberry-flavored cake has an ice cream filling.
   3) One cake has chocolate chips on top.
   4) The cake with one layer does not have chocolate chips on top.
   5) The cake with two layers has no filling

Based only on the information above, which of the following MUST be true?
   F. Oliver's cake has chocolate chips on top.
   G. Oliver's cake has an ice cream filling.
   H. Oswald's cake has chocolate chips on top.
   J. Oswald's cake has two layers.
   K. Cannot be determined from the information given

7. Whenever Vincent, Jules, Winston, and Jimmy work together, they always drink different types of coffee. The coffee types include cinnamon, decaf, French vanilla, and hazelnut.

1) Winston drinks cinnamon coffee.
2) Jimmy does not drink decaf or hazelnut coffee.
3) Vincent does not drink hazelnut or French vanilla coffee.

Which kind of coffee does Jules drink?
A. cinnamon
B. decaf
C. French vanilla
D. hazelnut
E. Cannot be determined from the information given.

8. Because the tomatoes Alice included in her salad did not come from the supermarket, she must have grown them herself.

Which of the following pieces of additional information makes it possible to determine that she grew the tomatoes herself?
F. Alice grows tomatoes in her garden.
G. Home-grown tomatoes are of higher quality than those sold at the supermarket.
H. Tomatoes from other stores are of lower quality than those sold at the supermarket.
J. Alice prefers to serve home-grown, organic food.
K. There are no accessible food stores near Alice besides the supermarket.

Questions 9 and 10 refer to the following information.

In the code below, (1) each letter represents the same word in every sentence, (2) each word is always represented by only one letter, and (3) in any given sentence, the letters may or may not be presented in the same order as the words.

T	**K**	**N**	**J**	**R**	means
"John	writes	short	mystery	stories."	
X	**N**	**J**	**R**	**S**	means
"John	reads	long	mystery	stories."	
P	**C**	**S**	**X**	**J**	means
"Jerry	reads	long	romance	stories."	
J	**X**	**R**	**P**	**T**	means
"Jerry	writes	long	mystery	stories."	
S	**L**	**P**	**M**	**K**	means
"Jerry	reads	short	western	novels."	

9. Which letter represents the word "mystery"?

    A. N
    B. J
    C. R
    D. X
    E. S

10. Which word is represented by the letter T?

    F. John
    G. stories
    H. long
    J. writes
    K. mystery

TEST EIGHT SOLUTIONS

1. **C** Create a chart with one column for each lunch type and one row for each characteristic: lunch owner and food type. Start by filling in the information you know based on Rule 1: Dermot's lunch is on the far left. Rule 2 tells you that Andy's lunch is 2 spaces to the right of the sandwich. Since there is one lunch between them, the sandwich must either be in Position 1 or 2. How can you determine which? Since Rule 3 tells you that the pork chop is to the left of the sandwich, the sandwich cannot be on the far left. You can now fill in the locations of the pork chop, the sandwich, and Andy's position.

Dermot			Andy
Pork chop	sandwich		

Only two names remain. Since Rule 4 tells us that Corinna's lunch is to the right of Bertrand's, you can fill in both names. Finally, only two lunch items are not filled in. Since Rule 4 states that the salad is not Corinna's, it must belong to Andy. Thus the casserole belongs to Corinna.

Dermot	Bertrand	Corinna	Andy
Pork chop	Sandwich	Casserole	salad

2. **F** Option A is correct because the question states that only some New Yorkers were born in New York City. This means that there are other New Yorkers who were not born in New York City. Option B is incorrect because it is not necessarily true that all New Yorkers were born in New York City. Option C is incorrect because only some New Yorkers actually live in New York City; there are other New Yorkers living in different parts of New York State. Options D and E can be ruled out because there is no information in the question to support them.

3. **C** The correct answer must be the contrapositive, which is formed by reversing and negating the two clauses. The contrapositive must be correct because it is the only other statement that cannot be argued against. This is represented by Option C. Option D is an assumption that cannot be supported by the information provided. All the other options are incorrect because they fail to rearrange the conditions into the contrapositive form.

4. **K** Option K is correct because it is the only possible conclusion one could make provided the given information is true. Option F is incorrect because, while this information makes it more likely that she went to an ATM, she could have gotten the cash from some other source. Option G is incorrect because the frequency of her ATM visits tells us nothing about other possible cash sources. Option H is incorrect because she still could have gotten cash from another source. Option J is incorrect because, as with Option F, it does not prove that the cash came from an ATM.

5. **B** We know from the question that all pre-med students must take Advanced Chemistry. However, they must pass the Introductory class to be eligible. If Marissa were a pre-med major and passed Introductory Chemistry, she would then take Advanced Chemistry. But since a student not majoring in pre-med might take Introductory Chemistry without moving onto Advanced Chemistry, Option B is correct.

Option A is incorrect because it is possible that she passed Introductory Chemistry but chose not to take Advanced Chemistry. Option C is incorrect because if Marissa had taken Advanced Chemistry, we would know that she passed Introductory Chemistry. But since she did not take this class, we cannot be sure. Option D is incorrect because the fact that all pre-med students must take Advanced Chemistry does not mean that only pre-med students take the course. Option E is correct only if Marissa is a pre-med major, but she may not be.

6. **F**   Draw a diagram like the one below. Start with Rule 1, which states that Oliver's cake is vanilla-flavored, and Oswald's cake is strawberry-flavored. Next, move onto Rule 2, which states that the strawberry-flavored cake has an ice cream filling. This rule must be referring to Oswald's birthday cake. Rule 5 states that the cake with two layers has no filling. Because Oswald's cake has an ice cream filling in it, Oliver's cake must be the cake with two layers and no filling. If Oliver's cake is the cake with two layers, then Oswald's cake has one layer and does not have chocolate chips on top according to Rule 4. Oliver's cake than must have chocolate chips on top per Rule 3. The correct answer is Option F.

Oswald's Birthday Cake	Oliver's Birthday Cake
strawberry	vanilla
ice cream filling	no filling
no chocolate chips	chocolate chips
one layer	two layers

7. **D**   Draw a diagram like the one below. According to Rule 1, Winston drinks cinnamon coffee, so fill that in first. Rule 2 tells us that Jimmy does not drink decaf or hazelnut coffee. Therefore, he must drink French vanilla coffee. Rule 3 states that Vincent does not drink hazelnut, which means he must drink decaf. Therefore, Jules has to drink hazelnut coffee. Option D is correct.

Vincent	Jules	Winston	Jimmy
decaf	hazelnut	cinnamon	French vanilla

8. **K** The question suggests that if Alice served tomatoes, they must have either come from the supermarket or been homegrown. For this to be true, there must be no other stores from which she could have bought the tomatoes. This makes Option K correct. Option F is possible, but it does not result in a definite conclusion. All the other options are opinions that are not supported by the information provided and do not necessarily support the conclusion.

9. **C** The word "mystery" appears only in sentences 1, 2, and 4. Likewise, the letter R appears only in sentences 1, 2, and 4. The letter J appears above these sentences but also appears in sentence 3. The word "mystery" is not in sentence 3. Therefore, Option B can be ruled out. Option A is incorrect because N only appears in sentences 1 and 2. Option D is incorrect because X appears in sentences 2, 3, and 4. Option E is incorrect because S appears in sentences 2, 3, and 5.

10. **J** The letter T appears in sentences 1 and 4 only. The word "writes" also appears only in sentences 1 and 4. No other words or letters appear only in sentences 1 and 4.

TEST NINE

1. Emmy, Staci, Jamal, and Clive are waiting in line to buy ice cream cones. The ice cream truck offers four flavors: chocolate, vanilla, strawberry, and mint. Each person buys a different flavor.

    1) Jamal does not buy chocolate or vanilla ice cream.
    2) Staci buys mint ice cream.
    3) Clive buys either strawberry or chocolate ice cream.
    4) Emmy does not buy strawberry ice cream.

    Which ice cream flavor does Emmy buy?
    A. chocolate
    B. mint
    C. strawberry
    D. vanilla
    E. Cannot be determined from the information given.

2. If it snows more than twelve inches, then schools will be closed. If schools are closed, Rokas will stay home from work.

    Based only on the information above, which of the following MUST be true?
    F. If Rokas does not stay home from work, then it did not snow more than twelve inches.
    G. If Rokas does not stay home from work, then it will snow more than twelve inches.
    H. Rokas stays home from work only if it snows more than twelve inches.
    J. If schools are closed, then it has snowed more than twelve inches.
    K. If Rokas stays home from work, the schools are closed.

3. Five girls in a second-grade class line up for lunch.

    1) Sadie is somewhere behind Athena.
    2) Athena is behind Jade and directly in front of Beth, who is in front of Sadie.
    3) Rosie is between Jade and Athena.

    Who is in the third position?
    A. Sadie
    B. Athena
    C. Beth
    D. Jade
    E. Rosie

4. Martin was accepted to both Mannix University and Royston University. Mannix University is more academically challenging than Royston University. The only thing Martin prefers about Royston University is the school's more active social scene. Martin chose Mannix University.

    Based only on the information above, which of the following MUST be true?
    F. Martin values academic challenges over any other quality in a school.
    G. A good social scene is not Martin's highest priority in choosing a school.
    H. Academically challenging schools usually have a less vibrant social scene.
    J. Martin did not take cost into account when choosing a college.
    K. If Royston University were better academically, Martin would have gone there.

5. The Breuckelen Records music label plans to release 4 rock albums, 5 pop albums, and 3 classical albums this year. They never release albums of the same genre in the same month. If Breuckelen Records releases no more than two albums per month and the first album they release is a rock album, what is the least number of months they will need to release all of the planned albums?

    A. 5
    B. 6
    C. 7
    D. 8
    E. 9

Questions 6 and 7 refer to the following information.

In the code below, (1) each letter represents the same word in every sentence, (2) each word is always represented by only one letter, and (3) in any given sentence, the letters may or may not be presented in the same order as the words.

T	**X**	**C**	**K**	**R**	means
"Sally	loves	good	romantic	movies."	
K	**X**	**G**	**R**	**N**	means
"Sally	like	good	dramatic	movies."	
Y	**D**	**T**	**X**	**K**	means
"Sally	loves	great	mystery	movies."	
V	**C**	**K**	**X**	**H**	means
"Sally	hates	bad	romantic	movies."	
G	**K**	**R**	**F**	**X**	means
"Sally	likes	good	funny	movies."	

6. Which word is represented by the letter T?

    F. Sally
    G. loves
    H. movies
    J. great
    K. romantic

7. Which letter represents the word "Sally"?

    A. T
    B. X
    C. K
    D. G
    E. Cannot be determined from the information given.

8. Five items are hanging in a closet: a sweater, a raincoat, a jacket, a vest, and a cape. Their owners are Vera, Wendell, Xenia, and Zane. One person owns two items.

   1) The cape is on the far right and is Vera's.
   2) The item on the far left is Wendell's.
   3) There is one item to the right of the raincoat but to the left of the sweater.
   4) The jacket is three positions to the right of Wendell's item.
   5) The vest and jacket belong to the same person.
   6) Xenia does not own the vest.

Who owns the vest?
   F. Vera
   G. Wendell
   H. Xenia
   J. Zane
   K. Cannot be determined from the information given.

9. Virginia sees a car in the employee parking lot. Because she knows that her co-workers Bob, Jim, and Doug have gone home, Virginia concludes that the car must belong to a woman.

Which of the following pieces of additional information makes it possible to determine that the car belongs to a woman?

    A. There are other men besides Bob, Jim, and Doug working with Virginia.

    B. Bob, Jim, and Doug are the only men who work with Virginia.

    C. Bob, Jim, and Doug own cars.

    D. Virginia works with more women than men.

    E. Everyone who works with Virginia owns a car.

10. All burgers are patties. Some patties are vegetarian. No vegetarian burgers contain any beef. Some beef patties contain diced vegetables.

Based only on the information above, which of the following MUST be true?

    F. All beef patties containing diced vegetables are vegetarian burgers.

    G. A beef patty can never contain diced vegetables.

    H. All burgers are either beef or vegetarian.

    J. Even if a beef patty contains diced vegetables, it is not a vegetarian burger.

    K. Cannot be determined from the information given.

TEST NINE ANSWERS

1. **D** Draw a diagram like the one below. First, fill in the fact that Staci buys mint ice cream according to Rule 2. Rule 1 tells us that Jamal does not buy either the chocolate or vanilla ice cream flavors. This means he must have ordered the strawberry ice cream. Rule 3 tells us that Clive orders either chocolate or strawberry ice cream. Since we now know that Jamal orders the strawberry flavor, we can deduce that Clive orders the chocolate ice cream. This means that Emmy orders the vanilla ice cream, which is Option D:

Emmy	Staci	Jamal	Clive
Vanilla	Mint	Strawberry	Chocolate

2. **F** Start by combining the two sentences:

"If it snows more than twelve inches, then schools will be closed, and Rokas will stay home from work."

Next, flip the conditions and negate them. You have just formed the contrapositive. Option F is the only answer choice that fulfills the conditions of the contrapositive. All the other answer choices are assumptions that are not supported by the information provided.

3. **B**   Draw a diagram for each rule to keep the information organized. Rule 1 states that Sadie is somewhere in line behind Athena.

Athena   →   Sadie

Rule 2 gives us more information to work with. This rule tells us that Athena is between Jade and Beth and that Beth is in front of Sadie. Now we can fill out the diagram further:

Jade   →   Athena   →   Beth   →   Sadie

We still don't have the complete order, however. Rule 3 tells us that Rosie is between Jenny and Athena:

Jade   →   Rosie   →   Athena   →   Beth   →   Sadie

Thus Athena is third in line.

4. **G**   The question tells us that Royston University has a better social scene and Mannix University has more challenging academics. However, the question does not give us the other circumstances that may have factored into Martin's decision. The fact that Royston University has a more active social scene indicates that social life is not his highest priority. Thus Option G is the best answer. Option F might be true, but there is not enough information to support it. Option H is an assumption that is not supported by the information provided. Option J is incorrect because, since we do not know whether Mannix University is more expensive than Royston University, we cannot be sure whether he took the cost into account. Option K is incorrect because Royston University may have other drawbacks that caused Martin not to go there.

5. **B**   Start by drawing a diagram like the one below. The question tells us that the rock albums are released first. Mark off the first four columns accordingly for the first four months. Now, one possibility for the rest of the diagram is to have the first classical album released in Month 1 along with the first rock album. As a result, they can start releasing the pop albums from Month 2 through Month 6. You should have five X's going across the Pop row from Months 2 to 6.

As the record company cannot release more than two albums each month, this leaves Months 5 and 6 for the remaining two classical albums. Mark the final two X's into these two columns. Your chart should look something like this:

	1	2	3	4	5	6	7
Rock	X	X	X	X			
Pop		X	X	X	X	X	
Classical	X				X	X	

Remember that the question is asking for the arrangement that gives us the **LEAST** number of months to release all of the planned albums. The correct answer is 6 months.

6. **G**   The letter T appears in sentences 1 and 3 but not in sentences 2, 4, or 5. The word "loves" is the only word that appears in sentences 1 and 3 but none of the other sentences. Option A can be ruled out because "Sally" appears in sentences 2 and 4 as well as 1 and 3. Option C is incorrect because "movies" appears in all 5 sentences. Option D can be eliminated because "great" appears only in sentence 3 and not in sentence 1. Option E is incorrect because "romantic" appears in sentences 1 and 4 but not in sentences 1 and 3.

7. **E** "Sally" appears in all five sentences. The word "movies" also appears in all five sentences. The letters X and K also appear in all five sentences. Nothing in the code allows you to determine whether X or K represents "Sally."

8. **J** Start by drawing a diagram with one row for the item types and one for the owners' names. Next, write in what you already know based on Rules 1 and 2: Vera and her cape are on the far right, and Wendell is to the far left.

Wendell				Vera
				cape

Next, look at Rule 4. This rule states that the jacket is three positions to the right of Wendell's item. Find Wendell in the chart and count three spaces to the right and fill the space with the jacket.

Wendell				Vera
			jacket	cape

Now look at Rule 3. This rule states that there is one item to the right of the raincoat but to the left of the sweater. This means that this unknown item is between the raincoat and the sweater. As such, the raincoat must belong to Wendell and the sweater must be to the left of the jacket.

Wendell				Vera
raincoat		sweater	jacket	cape

The only item missing from our chart is the vest, which goes between the raincoat and the sweater.

Wendell				Vera
raincoat	vest	sweater	jacket	cape

Rule 6 states that Xenia is not the owner of the vest. If she is not the owner of the vest, then she is also not the owner of the jacket since Rule 5 tells us that the same person owns both the vest and the jacket. The only remaining item is the sweater which must be Xenia's. That leaves Zane as the owner of the vest and the jacket. Option J is the correct answer.

Wendell	Zane	Xenia	Zane	Vera
raincoat	Vest	sweater	jacket	cape

9. **B**   Virginia's conclusion is that the car belongs to a woman because Bob, Jim, and Doug already left. This would only make sense if no other men worked at this office; otherwise, the car could belong to anyone. The only answer choice that supports this conclusion is Option B. Option A makes the conclusion less likely because if other men work with Virginia, the car could belong to a man. Option C introduces information that is irrelevant to the question. Option D indicates that she works with other men who could also own the car. Option E tells us nothing about the gender of the car's owner.

10. **J**   Option F can be ruled out because the question states that no vegetarian burgers contain any beef. Option G is an opinion that is not stated anywhere in the question. Option H is a generalization; some burgers are made from turkey, while other burgers are made from tofu. Option J is the correct answer because it is consistent with the information provided. According to the question, a vegetarian burger cannot contain any beef no matter what.

—————— TEST TEN

1. Jim visits a showroom while shopping for a new car. All new cars in the showroom are hard tops. Some cars have automatic transmissions, while others use stick shifts. Convertibles are also being sold in the showroom. No convertible in the showroom has a hard top.

   Based only on the information above, which of the following MUST be true?

   A. Jim's new car must be a hard top.
   B. If Jim buys a convertible at the showroom, it must be a used car.
   C. If Jim buys a new hard top car, he must have bought it at the showroom.
   D. The showroom sells hard top cars because they are safer than convertibles.
   E. More cars shown at the showroom have automatic transmissions than stick shifts.

2. Gina went to the movie theater with a friend. They watched two movies.

   1) One movie was a documentary, and the other movie was a drama.
   2) One of the movies is in black-and-white and is 120 minutes long.
   3) One of the movies is 90 minutes long and is being shown in 3D.
   4) The movie that is being shown in 2D is not in color.
   5) The documentary is in color.

   Based only on the information above, which of the following MUST be true?

   F. The drama is 90 minutes long.
   G. The documentary is being shown in 2D.
   H. The documentary is 120 minutes long.
   J. The documentary is being shown in 3D.
   K. Cannot be determined from the information given.

3. If Karen plays tennis at camp, then Joe plays soccer. If Joe plays soccer at camp, then Ross goes swimming.

    Based only on the information above, which of the following MUST be true?
    A. If Ross does not go swimming, then Karen is not playing tennis.
    B. If Ross goes swimming, then Joe plays soccer.
    C. If Joe plays soccer, then Karen plays tennis.
    D. If Karen does not play tennis, then Joe does not play soccer.
    E. If Joe does not play soccer, then Ross does not go swimming.

4. Six books are lined up from left to right on top of a desk. Three of these books belong to Marcia, and three belong to Greg. The books include a novel, a textbook, a comic book, a dictionary, a poetry book, and a self-help book.

    1) The self-help book is on the far right.
    2) There are two books between the dictionary and the self-help book.
    3) None of Greg's books are next to each other.
    4) The dictionary belongs to Marcia.
    5) There are three books between the poetry book and the comic book.
    6) The novel is to the left of the textbook and the comic book.

    Which three books belong to Marcia?
    F. novel, textbook, self-help book
    G. poetry book, novel, dictionary
    H. poetry book, dictionary, comic book
    J. textbook, comic book, self-help book
    K. novel, textbook, comic book

5. Noah bounced five different balls against the floor to determine how high each one would bounce. He ranked the five balls from highest to lowest according to the height of each ball's bounce.

    1) The tennis ball bounced lower than the golf ball.
    2) The soccer ball bounced higher than the football.
    3) The baseball bounced lower than the tennis ball.
    4) The soccer ball had the 4th highest bounce.

In which position is the tennis ball?
    A. first
    B. second
    C. third
    D. fourth
    E. fifth

6. Every year Professor Callahan awards a special internship to one student in his class. The winning student must have maintained an average of at least a B+. Warner wanted the internship and earned an A in the class, but Professor Callahan awarded the internship to Elle.

Based only on the information above, which of the following MUST be true?
    F. Elle received a B+ or higher in the class.
    G. Elle received an A or higher in the class.
    H. Grades are the most important factor in awarding the internship.
    J. If Warner had earned a higher grade, then he would have received the internship.
    K. Some factor other than grades is most important for awarding the internship.

Questions 7 and 8 refer to the following information.

In the code below, (1) each letter represents the same word in every sentence, (2) each word is always represented by only one letter, and (3) in any given sentence, the letters may or may not be presented in the same order as the words.

K	T	W	G	V	means
"Luke	enjoys	eating	hot	sandwiches."	

T	N	W	X	G	means
"Luke	dislikes	eating	cold	sandwiches."	

P	M	X	T	K	means
"Luke	enjoys	drinking	cold	tea."	

N	P	V	M	R	means
"Harvey	dislikes	drinking	hot	tea."	

G	X	N	C	T	means
"Luke	dislikes	eating	cold	soup."	

7. Which word is represented by the letter T?

    A. sandwiches
    B. enjoys
    C. cold
    D. Luke
    E. Cannot be determined from the information given.

8. Which letter represents the word "soup"?

    F. T
    G. N
    H. X
    J. C
    K. Cannot be determined from the information given.

9. Some campaign workers went to the candidate's early morning meeting. None of the campaign workers arrived on time.

Based only on the information above, which of the following MUST be true?
   A. Saskia was late for the meeting so she must be a campaign worker.
   B. Usman is a campaign worker, and he arrived early for the meeting so he could go home early.
   C. Yuko is a campaign worker, and she was late to the meeting.
   D. Rocky did not attend the meeting, so he is not a campaign worker.
   E. Desiree did not attend the meeting, so she no longer supports the candidate.

10. Dani tried to mow her lawn yesterday. She discovered her lawnmower was stolen. Her lawn has still not been mowed.

Based only on the information above, which of the following MUST be true?
   F. Dani's lawn is becoming overgrown.
   G. Lawnmowers are expensive to replace.
   H. Dani can hire someone else to mow the lawn.
   J. Dani always promptly mows her lawn unless something gets in her way.
   K. Dani did not hire anyone else to mow her lawn.

TEST TEN SOLUTIONS

1. **B** Since all new cars shown in the showroom are hard tops, and no convertible in the showroom has a hard top, it follows that any convertible Jim purchased there must be a used car. Thus Option B is correct. Option A is incorrect because it doesn't consider that Jim may have bought either a new car or a used one. Option C can be ruled out because he may have bought this type of car elsewhere. Options D and E are assumptions that are not supported by the information provided.

2. **J** Draw a diagram so you can keep the information about the two movies organized. Start with Rule 5, which tells us that the documentary is in color. Next, refer to Rule 2. This rule states that the film in black-and-white is also 120 minutes long. This rule must be referring to the drama. Rule 3 states that one of the movies is 90 minutes long and is being shown in 3D. This has to be referring to the documentary. According to Rule 4, the movie being shown in 2D is not in color, which means that the black-and-white drama is the 2D film. The correct answer is Option D:

Documentary	Drama
Color	Black-and-White
90 Minutes	120 Minutes
3D	2D

3. **A** Combine the statements into one "If/Then" clause: "If Karen plays tennis at camp, then Joe plays soccer and Ross goes swimming." The contrapositive is formed by reversing the clauses and negating both of them. Option A is correct because it fulfills the conditions of the contrapositive. Because none of the other options are presented in the contrapositive form, they are not necessarily true and therefore can be ruled out.

4. **H** Draw a diagram with six columns (one column for each book) and two rows (one for the book types and one for the owners). Write in the location of the self-help book. Since there are two books between the self-help book and the dictionary, you can now determine the dictionary's location. Rule 4 states that the dictionary belongs to Marcia. Next, look at Rule 3: None of Greg's books are next to each other. Since each person has 3 books, they must alternate on the shelf according to the owner. This means that if you know the owner and location of one book, you can fill in the rest of the row:

		Dictionary			Self-help book
Marcia	Greg	Marcia	Greg	Marcia	Greg

Now look at Rule 5, which states that there are three books between the poetry book and the comic book. These books must be in Positions 1 and 5. However, we do not yet know which book is in Position 1 or Position 5. Since the novel is to the left of the comic book, the comic book is in Position 5 and the poetry book is in Position 1. To determine the locations of the remaining books, note that the novel is to the left of the textbook:

Poetry book	Novel	Dictionary	Textbook	Comic book	Self-help book
Marcia	Greg	Marcia	Greg	Marcia	Greg

5. **B**   Draw a diagram for each rule to keep the information organized. Rule 1 tells us that the tennis ball bounced lower than the golf ball:

golf ball

↓

tennis ball

Rule 2 tells us that the soccer ball bounced higher than the football:

soccer ball

↓

football

Rule 4 tells us that the soccer ball had the 4th highest bounce. This means that the football had the lowest bounce. We also know that the golf ball had either the first or second highest bounce. In addition, we know that the tennis ball had either the second or third highest bounce depending on where the baseball's bounce height ranks.

Finally, Rule 3 tells us that the baseball bounced lower than the tennis ball. This means that the baseball had the third highest bounce because the soccer ball had the fourth highest bounce; moreover, the football bounced lower than the soccer ball. This means that the golf ball had the highest bounce, and the tennis ball had the second highest bounce.

The question is asking us for the tennis ball's position, which we know to be the second highest. Option B is the correct answer.

6. **F** The student who receives the internship must have at least a B+ average. Since Elle won the internship, she must have earned at least a B+ average. Thus Option F is correct. Option G is incorrect because without knowing that the internship is based solely on grades, we cannot conclude that Elle's grade was higher than Warner's. Option H is incorrect because the question does not state whether there are other factors involved in the decision. Option J is incorrect because Warner may have received a higher grade than Elle but lost the internship for some other reason. Option K is incorrect because it is possible that the internship is based only on grades, and that Elle simply received the highest grade.

7. **D** The letter T appears in sentences 1, 2, 3, and 5. The word "Luke" also appears in sentences 1, 2, 3 and 5. No other word or letter appears in these four sentences alone.

8. **J** The word "soup" appears only in sentence 5. The letter C also appears only in sentence 5. There are no other letters or words that only appear in sentence 5.

9. **C** The question states that only some campaign workers attended the candidate's early morning meeting. This means that some of the other campaign workers missed it. This rules out Option A. While Saskia was late to the meeting; it is not necessarily true that she is a campaign worker. She could serve some other function within the campaign, other than that of a campaign worker. Option B is incorrect because the question states nothing about campaign workers being allowed to go home early. Option D is incorrect because we don't have enough information to determine whether or not Rocky is a campaign worker. Option E is flawed because Desiree may have had other reasons for why she didn't attend the meeting. This leaves us with Option C, which is correct. If Yuko went to the meeting as a campaign worker, she couldn't have arrived on time because the question states that none of them did.

10. **K** We know that Dani's lawn has not yet been mowed. If she had hired some-one else to do it, the lawn would be mowed by now. Thus we can conclude that she did not hire anyone else to do it. This makes Option K the best an-swer. Option F is an opinion that is not necessarily true because Dani could have been planning to mow the lawn long before it became overgrown. Op-tion G is irrelevant to the question. Option H is incorrect because if the lawn is not mowed, then we cannot conclude that she can simply hire someone else to do it. Option J is invalid because we know nothing about what Dani normally does.

Made in the USA
Middletown, DE
05 January 2022